Mining for God's Gold in Life's Dark Valleys

Margaret E. Head

ONESTONE

BIBLICAL RESOURCES

Published by:
One Stone Press
979 Lovers Lane
Bowling Green, KY 42103

Printed in the United States of America

All biblical references are based upon the
New American Standard Bible.

ISBN: 978-1-941422-58-8

ONE STONE
BIBLICAL RESOURCES
www.onestone.com

Contents

"Teach me, O Lord, the way of Your statutes,
And I shall observe it to the end.
Give me understanding, that I may observe Your law
And keep it with all my heart."
—Psalm 119:33-34

Acknowledgments

The scriptures referenced in this book are taken from the New American Standard Bible, except for a few passages I have chosen from the Zondervan New International Version. As a tribute to the Holy Trinity, I have taken the liberty to capitalize Their Names in the scriptures I have chosen to quote from the NIV.

All poetry has been written by the author unless acknowledged otherwise.

Included are also several hymns written by men and women who have embraced the love of God in their hearts. May their comforting, scripturally inspired thoughts help us as we seek the peace our loving God extends to His servants. "Let the word of Christ richly dwell within you, with all wisdom teaching and admonishing one another with psalms and hymns and spiritual songs, singing with thankfulness in your hearts to God" (Colossians 3:16).

The help with content, and the consistent encouragement provided by two caring sisters, Paula Hovater and Summer Mauldin, are very much responsible for the emotional energy needed to finish this task. Adequately expressing my appreciation to them would be an impossible undertaking.

Also, with deepest gratitude for their valuable help in making the publication of this book possible, I would like to acknowledge the following people:

My appreciation to my son, Mark, for designing the beautiful and fitting cover, for preliminary and final proofing, formatting, and the necessary preparation for final production. His regular work requires many long hours and I am very grateful for his help.

To my daughter, Marsha, for her encouragement, input, and assistance in proofreading, even as she mines for gold in her own frequent and long dark valleys. She ultimately fills them with overflowing joy for being privileged to serve in God's vineyard.

5

To David Maxson and Gary Henry, preachers of the Gospel; God's faithful servants, and my brothers in the Lord. Both give daily encouragement, not only by their examples of servitude, but also with regular posts. Both have very kindly allowed me to quote them in this book.

To Nel Hazelwood, sister of my son-in-law, and also my sister in Christ, who has helped and encouraged me with useful suggestions, proofreading, and in many other time-consuming ways. I, among many, many others, have had the privilege of personally being blessed by her very kind, meticulous "nursing care."

To Lii Ern Tan and Janna Shannon for tirelessly helping with essential corrections and suggestions. Lii's computer knowledge and skills were critical throughout the entire project.

And to all who have given me encouragement as I work to clarify God's expectations of His children as we find ourselves in troublesome situations: my sister and close friend, Cean Johnson, was first to request "another book." The valleys she has personally dealt with have been numerous, painfully long and difficult: yet today, her loyalty to Godly service is firm and undiminished, a beautiful example of steadfast servitude.

After prayerfully searching God's Word together, we will find there is indeed an abundance of priceless pure gold in it if we open our hearts and minds while chipping away prideful "selfish self" to receive and embrace it. If applied to our lives, these saving nuggets from the mind of God can assist us in finding the gateway to His throne of grace and eventually to His eternal new Jerusalem, His Holy Mountain!

> *"It is good for me that I was afflicted,*
> *That I may learn Your statutes.*
> *The law of Your mouth is better to me*
> *Than thousands of gold and silver pieces."*
> *—Psalm 119:71-72*

Dedication

To my very close friends, Rodney and Paula Hovater, who are always just a phone call away, willing and eager to help in any way possible, even while dealing with inevitable valleys of their own. I cannot begin to enumerate the ways they have chosen to serve God. They spend their daily lives reaching out to others (including myself) who are nourished and comforted by their extreme kindness. God has blessed me richly with their loving friendship!

To my beloved children, Marsha Hazelwood, Mark Head, and Marsha's husband Walter; and my grandchildren and great-grandchildren. They are God's precious gift to me. May we always serve Him steadfastly.

To Ross and Nancy Fink: gentle, kind, loving, and firm in the Lord; they are God's loyal, dedicated servants who help care for and feed His sheep, both physically and spiritually. Nancy has authored a valuable classroom workbook (Minor Prophets) that can be purchased online from One Stone Bookstore and Amazon. Ross has preached and continues to preach the Word of God so very humbly and capably.

To Seth and Summer Mauldin, who are fervently working to find and save the lost and strengthen the faithful. Seth has a special desire to encourage young men who are preaching or learning to preach and have a burning desire to grow in the knowledge of the Truth. He not only does this in the area where he lives but also assists with teaching at the Rustic Youth Camp in Belgreen, Alabama. Their zeal to be productive servants of God is outstanding. Summer has authored a valuable book for young mothers, A Home of Hope, available on Amazon. Proceeds from sales assist a couple with the expense of adopting a baby.

To Jarred and Katie McCrary, another outstanding young couple who have a deep interest in training young students to remain faithful to God, especially throughout the very difficult teenage years. Jarred is a very capable minister for the South Cullman Church of Christ and assists with teaching at the Rustic Youth Camp and other avenues.

To Jackie and Bunny Richardson, who were co-founders of the Rustic Youth Camp. Jackie has served as a preacher and teacher of the Gospel in many states and continues to serve with fervor as his strength allows.

An exciting and much-needed addition to the youth camp is now in progress.

To Robert and Arline Harkrider, who have published many books and an abundance of valuable teaching material. They have also edited many, many manuscripts for others, and reviewed my material: they are a valuable and precious gift to me! Robert is a very effective preacher and teacher of the Gospel, an elder for the Roswell Church of Christ, and a much-sought-after counselor concerning spiritual matters.

To David and Flora Tant, who have traveled to Jamaica, Malaysia, the Philippines, and other parts of the world, risking their own lives to spread God's precious, soul-saving word. Their success in this area of God's work is phenomenal.

And, also to Sewell Hall, who is like-minded in serving God, both here and abroad. Sewell was also involved in founding the Rustic Youth Camp.

To David and Anna Laura Norfleet, who also are of the same Christlike mind and have also served here and abroad in sharing the Gospel with others.

To Anita Turner, wife of Allan Turner (now deceased), another sister in Christ. Allan taught God's word to many students, both in their home, the pulpit, and abroad. Anita has faithfully carried out the role of being his most worthy companion in the Lord. She continues to manage sales of his excellent religious books that may be purchased from Allanita Press Publishing at 585 Cox Road Roswell, Georgia 30075.

And finally, to Buddy Payne, President of Florida College, and preacher of the Gospel, who has dedicated his life to serving our young men and women at a most crucial time in their lives. The college serves to strengthen them spiritually while giving them the very best education available. He is very ably and lovingly supported in his work by his faithful wife, Marilyn.

All the above preachers and teachers of the Gospel could have books written about themselves; but they would care for none of that. Their burning desire is to find their names written in the Lamb's Book of Life!

*"HOW BEAUTIFUL ARE THE FEET OF THOSE WHO BRING
GOOD NEWS OF GOOD THINGS!"*
—Romans 10:15b

*"And the ransomed of the Lord will return
And come with joyful shouting to Zion,
With everlasting joy upon their heads.
They will find gladness and joy,
And sorrow and sighing will flee away."*
—Isaiah 35:10

Commendation

As infants, we begin this earthly journey with childish trust and love, confidently expecting others to show the same warm, comforting love toward us.

However, in time we sin, and others sin against us, and disappointment and discouragement fill our young hearts. We eventually realize if we are to persevere, we must search for a dependable, permanent place of secure trust. Studying God's Holy Scriptures assures us with the same trust we enjoyed as a child and renews us when we are "born again" (through baptism) into His, Christ established, church: God's family of believers. Our love for and our trust in Him can, at last, be permanently secure.

In time, sin leaves a condemned mark on our soul, leaving us with the urgent need to be cleansed and made new again. Through His Word, we find cleansing is possible if we obediently repent, confess, and pray for forgiveness. The priceless gold nuggets in God's Word will then have brought us back to that same saved man or woman we were before sin reentered our life.

Ms. Margaret, as she is known to all, shares some of the wisdom she has learned over a lifetime to help us persevere, even when we have allowed Satan or others to place us in deep, painful valleys. She helps us deal with the tragedies of life that none will escape. Living brings its tears and hardships, but she helps us understand that God's grace is sufficient for us, and His unlimited power is made perfect in our weakness. Paul, the apostle, could boast concerning his weakness, "so that the power of Christ may dwell in me" (2 Corinthians 12:9b). —Michael Moore, Atlanta, Ga.

The gospel offers freedom from sin to everyone who will hear the message. So the call to "repent" is based on the gracious offer of forgiveness, in light of the gracious warning that someday, those who refuse the offer will perish in judgment

So how do we change the disposition and purpose of our hearts? We acknowledge the rule of the King in our lives. We stop seeing ourselves and our desires as our guides. We experience a fundamental shift in who we are, to see God as absolutely true and beautiful and worthy of all our adoration and obedience. If we fervently meditate on and embrace this spiritual reality, all of the hard stuff will become easy stuff, and we will "bear fruit in keeping with repentance" (Matthew 3:8). That's the Lord's will for every soul on earth. —Joshua Carter

"My little children, I am writing these things to you
so that you may not sin.
And if anyone sins, we have an Advocate with the Father,
Jesus Christ the righteous;
and He Himself is the propitiation (or satisfaction) for our sins;
and not for ours only, but also for those of the whole world."
—1 John 2:1-2

Foreword

I have selected scriptures to remind each of us to consider, and perhaps reconsider, how we respond to the seemingly inescapable valleys that come into our lives.

"This is my comfort in my affliction,
That Your word has revived me."
—Psalms 119:50

Throughout the book, you will read about the experiences of others who have mined or are continuing to mine their own painful, challenging valleys. May their Godly examples serve as beacons of light to help us in our quest to keep our love for God and His Word safely intact and the salvation of our oft endangered souls our primary focus. May we fully appreciate their willingness to recall and relate their very painful personal experiences so that we might grow in strength and perseverance.

Ernesto and Michelle Negron

Ernesto and Michelle Negron are continuing to mine in their deep valley of grief after the loss of their twelve-year-old son to brain cancer. The pain of their excruciating loss is ongoing, and their precious son will remain in their hearts throughout their lifetime; but their love for, and their faith in, God is forever strong and undiminished. They live on, lovingly and unselfishly serving God and their fellow man with renewed, loving fervor. They, like King David of old, wait patiently to be reunited  with their son in God's New Jerusalem. At the end of chapter three, you will be able to read an inspiring account of a faithful mother's life of godly perseverance.

Tony, Rhonda, and David Ditter

David Ditter shares his and his wife, Rhonda's, struggle to overcome her metastatic cancer and their unfailing determination to persevere in their service to God. Inserted throughout the book, you will be able to read journal entries detailing how they valiantly fought the good fight of faith even during the darkest hours of emotional and physical suffering.

Michael Moore

Michael Moore allows us to feel his bitter, heartbreaking emotions after his wife deserted him for a younger man. This was not a comfortable, feel-good revelation of his very personal feelings. He was willing to contribute this account only as a learning experience for others who need encouragement while in a valley, especially concerning marriage or divorce. You will find this exceedingly emotional, spiritual trial recorded near the close of chapter five.

Ruby and Bruce Hall

Ruby Hall shares her response to the loss of her husband Bruce, her mate, her joy, and her rock in times of stress. This account can also be found near the close of chapter five.

These broken families are experiencing triumph and joy through a deep abiding faith and commitment to God.

"I press on toward the goal for the prize
of the upward call of God in Christ Jesus."
—Philippians 3:14

Chapter 1

Why Our Painful Earthly Valleys Are to be Treasured

A few years ago, I was recovering from a painful fall in a local rehabilitation center. The care was excellent, and the staff and management very efficient, but it was there I became deeply concerned that many of the patients were experiencing feelings of deep depression and hopelessness. It was sadly apparent many of them were missing the love and comfort of God that can be found in the holy scriptures. I am writing this book to provide easy access to some of those particularly comforting, reassuring scriptures.

Reading this book is not meant to replace or to satisfy the need to read the Bible, but only to give an easy path to scriptures that address escaping from these dark valleys. The Bible was written under the direction and guidance of the Holy Spirit of God! No other book has ever been, or ever will be written that compares to it. I have lived for nearly ninety-five years, and it is because of His Holy Word I have been able to endure and escape the many excruciating valleys of my own. And yes, I now highly treasure what I have learned from each of them, and I would be remiss if I did not thank God for them. It is my wish that through these comforting passages the reader will feel His abundant love and abiding peace in every chapter.

Will we ever completely understand everything we might like to know about God's plans for His creation while we are on this earth? Probably not.

*"The secret things belong to the LORD our God,
but the things revealed belong to us and to our
sons forever, that we may observe all the words
of this law."
—Deuteronomy 29:29*

However, we can live joyfully, safely content with what He has revealed.

> *"All Scripture is inspired by God*
> *and profitable for teaching, for reproof,*
> *for correction, for training in righteousness;*
> *so that the man of God may be adequate,*
> *equipped for every good work."*
> —2 Timothy 3:16-17

> *"Grace and peace be multiplied to you*
> *in the knowledge of God and of Jesus*
> *our Lord; seeing that His divine power*
> *has granted to us everything pertaining*
> *to life and godliness, through the true*
> *knowledge of Him who called us by His*
> *own glory and excellence."*
> —2 Peter 1:2-3

The knowledge of God and Jesus multiplies grace and peace to us. Is it that my peace is lacking because of my failure to study His word adequately?

As we contemplate the following Biblical events surrounding Job, Peter, Paul, and other faithful servants of God, may we allow these accounts to show us how to turn deep sorrow and painful suffering into joy and extreme darkness into light. Though emotionally and many times physically painful, these trials provide a golden opportunity for us and those around us to grow spiritually and become more productive, insightful and caring servants.

How we walk through and mine our gold nuggets during periods of dark grief and stress is extremely important as our actions can, and do, encourage or discourage others. May each of us renew our zeal and our commitment to God to persevere faithfully as men and women of valor until we reach and pass through that last valley; joyfully, and unafraid to meet our Savior, Jesus the Christ, the Son of the Most-High God.

Often, God has allowed deep suffering in our lives to once more open our eyes that we have allowed to become blind to our very own spiritual inadequacies. *"Why do you look at the speck that is in your brother's eye, but do not notice the log that is in your own eye? Or how can you*

18

say to your brother, 'Brother, let me take out the speck that is in your eye,' when you yourself do not see the log that is in your own eye? You hypocrite, first take the log out of your own eye, and then you will see clearly to take out the speck that is in your brother's eye" (Luke 6:41-42).

Following is a confession of how my son John helped me remove a log that was in my own eye: One day while taking him to an appointment, he tossed this gold nugget out of his valley of bipolar depression to me as he said, "Mom, you can never admit you are wrong!" And he was right! I needed to hear this and change my attitude about always having to be right! I was grateful to him, and I am grateful to God for being enlightened and given the opportunity to grow spiritually.

You may ask if God places us in our valleys or if Satan alone is responsible (Ephesians 6:12). But it follows since God is ALL powerful, He may have allowed Satan enough power to place us there for testing purposes, as He did Job: or God Himself may have allowed the experience for our spiritual growth because sin had placed us there.

> "Therefore, those also who suffer according to the will of God
> shall entrust their souls to a faithful Creator in doing what is right."
> —1 Peter 4:19

All valleys are useful if we use them wisely to reconsider our present condition and redirect our steps with courage to follow more closely after Christ, or to encourage others who are struggling. Whether we are in a valley or not, God would have us understand that He does not tempt anyone: "*Blessed is a man who perseveres under trial; for once he has been approved, he will receive the crown of life which the Lord has promised to those who love Him. Let no one say when he is tempted, "I am being tempted by God"; for God cannot be tempted by evil, and He Himself does not tempt anyone. But each one is tempted when he is carried away and enticed by his own lust*" (James 1:12-14).

> Our God, the God of all goodness:
> Our God, the God of all grace!
> Worthy of greater love and highest praise,
> Even as deep, dark valleys we face.
>
> We need not falter as we run
> The race You have placed before us:

You will only allow what we can bear;
As in You alone, Our God, we place our trust!

In our quest to more fully understand God's revealed plan and purpose for us, we are privileged to review the response of some of God's most faithful, dedicated servants. And to then consider:

"Am I more righteous than they that
there should be no valleys of suffering in my life?"

According to secular history, Peter and Paul, two of Christ's loyal apostles, were martyred in Rome under the reign of Nero about 66 AD. Paul was beheaded, and Peter was crucified upside-down at his own request so that his death would not be in the same way his beloved and now exalted Savior had died. The other apostles (except John, the beloved) were also martyred. John spent time in prison on the small Isle of Patmos. Why were they willing to suffer in this way? Very clearly, it was because of their unfailing love for and steadfast belief in Jesus that they would not deny Him whom they trusted to welcome them into His everlasting, joyful dwelling place.

"Therefore, having been justified by faith,
we have peace with God through our Lord
Jesus Christ, through whom also we have
obtained our introduction by faith into this
grace in which we stand; and we exult in
hope of the glory of God. And not only
this, but we also exult in our tribulations,
knowing that tribulation brings about
perseverance; and perseverance, proven
character; and proven character, hope;
and hope does not disappoint, because
the love of God has been poured out
within our hearts through the Holy Spirit
who was given to us."
—Romans 5:1-5

Abundant, triumphant spiritual growth is waiting for those who mine their valleys and apply these "God-supplied" character-building nuggets to their lives.

*"I will rejoice and be glad in Your lovingkindness,
Because You have seen my affliction;
You have known the troubles of my soul."*
—Psalm 31:7

Paul relates this learning experience he endured: *"Because of the surpassing greatness of the revelations, for this reason, to keep me from exalting myself, there was given me a thorn in the flesh, a messenger of Satan to torment me–to keep me from exalting myself! Concerning this I implored the Lord three times that it might leave me. And He has said to me, 'My grace is sufficient for you, for power is perfected in weakness.' Most gladly, therefore, I will rather boast about my weaknesses, so that the power of Christ may dwell in me"* (2 Corinthians 12:7-9). Note Paul's willingness to accept this "messenger of Satan finally." When we pray to God for relief from a valley, are we willing to accept God's answer, as Paul was? I should be very careful about any complaining that will only confuse others concerning God's plan to do what is right and good for me. I must ask myself when I am tormented with pain, if I in my weakness, pain, or sorrow, am allowing the devil to turn me away from the final prize of heaven? (That is, of course, the devil's goal.) If so, I am allowing the devil to win! But in the day of judgment, both of us are destined to lose: *"Then He will also say to those on His left, 'Depart from Me, accursed ones, into the eternal fire which has been prepared for the devil and his angels"* (Matthew 25:41).

Can the cost of this loss be computed, or even compared to any physical or monetary loss we may experience while living on this earth? It is not humanly possible!

And Peter further reveals: *"Blessed be the God and Father of our Lord Jesus Christ, who according to His great mercy has caused us to be born again to a living hope through the resurrection of Jesus Christ from the dead, to obtain an inheritance which is imperishable and undefiled and will not fade away, reserved in heaven for you, who are protected by the power of God through faith for a salvation ready to be revealed in the last time. In this you greatly rejoice, even though now for a little while, if necessary, you have been distressed by various trials, so that the proof of your faith, being more precious than gold which is perishable, even though tested by fire, may be found to result in praise and glory and honor at the revelation of Jesus Christ; and though you have not seen Him, you love Him, and though you do not see Him* now, but believe in Him, you greatly rejoice with joy inexpressible and full of glory, obtaining as the outcome of your faith the salvation of your souls" (1Peter 1:3-9). "...according to my earnest expectation and hope, that I will not be put to shame in anything, but that with all boldness, Christ will even now, as always, be exalted in my body, whether by life or by death. For to me, to live is Christ and to die is gain" (Philippians 1:20-21). This New Testament book was written by the apostle Paul as the Holy Spirit guided him. And yes, Paul did, (as did the other apostles), die to gain! The following was penned by the apostle John, while in exile on the Isle of Patmos:

"And the wall of the city had twelve foundation stones,
and on them were the twelve names of the twelve apostles of the
Lamb."
—Revelation 21:14

"Consider it all joy, my brethren,
when you encounter various trials,
knowing that the testing of your faith produces endurance.
And let endurance have its perfect result, so that you
may be perfect and complete, lacking in nothing."
—James 1:2-4

And what is the *"perfect result"* of *"endurance"*? We can be *"perfect and complete, lacking in nothing"*! This valuable spiritual growth is the direct result of testing our faith. Faithful, tested and tormented, enduring Job gives us the powerful reason to be joyful while in our valleys: *"But it is still my consolation, and I rejoice in unsparing pain, That I have not denied the words of the Holy One" (Job 6:10).*

Have we learned to "consider it all joy" when we face these trials in our lives that are designed to bring us to perfection? If so, have we remembered to thank God for these valleys that have caused us to grow and to flourish? If not, are we failing the test? If we are content in being able to suffer for Christ, we will not be spending our time degrading those who have the rule over us, or even those who persecute us; but instead, we will be praying for the salvation of their souls through obedience to God's will.

"You have heard that it was said,
'YOU SHALL LOVE YOUR NEIGHBOR
and hate your enemy.' But I say to you, love
your enemies and pray for those who persecute
you, so that you may be sons of your Father who
is in heaven; for He causes His sun to rise on the
evil and the good, and sends rain on the
righteous and the unrighteous."
—Matthew 5:43-45

As I consider these scriptures, I am humbled and deeply grateful that I have a Father who is aware of my shortcomings and is lovingly helping me prepare for the second coming of His "exalted" Son.

"Do not let your heart be troubled;
believe in God, believe also in Me.
In My Father's house are many dwelling places;
if it were not so, I would have told you;
for I go to prepare a place for you.
If I go and prepare a place for you,
I will come again and receive you to Myself,
that where I am, there you may be also.
And you know the way where I am going."
Thomas said to Him,
"Lord, we do not know where You are going,
how do we know the way?"
Jesus said to him,
"I am the way, and the truth, and the life;
no one comes to the Father but through Me."
—John 14:1-6

Knowing this, it is urgent for us to continuously be found cleansed from sin and ready to be admitted into that glorious place prepared for His obedient children! A GIFT of God's grace we are not able to fully comprehend' and we can never, on our own, be worthy of that honor, but only through cleansing by the blood of His only begotten Son, Jesus the Christ!

Christ was willing to die on a demeaning bloody cross in obedience to His Father's will. Thus, through His unselfish, excruciatingly painful, humiliating example, He teaches us that heaven is worth even the cost of being forsaken by friends, reviled, spit upon, brutally beaten, and cruelly stripped of every sense of modesty, or put to death by hate-filled, mocking sinful men. And none of us can say we are without sin except for the blessed gift of His cleansing blood! No, not one! And yet, He suffered this for us! "If we say that we have no sin, we are deceiving ourselves and the truth is not in us" (1 John 1:8).

> *"Therefore as you have received*
> *Christ Jesus the Lord, so walk in Him,*
> *having been firmly rooted and now*
> *being built up in Him and established*
> *in your faith, just as you were instructed,*
> *and overflowing with gratitude."*
> *—Colossians 2:6-7*

Is my gratitude constantly overflowing for this gracious gift of love? Only I can answer that question. And how much gratitude is enough? More than I can ever express, but gratefully, God knows my limitations.

If you are old enough to read and understand this book, you may have already experienced the dark valley of deep grief that we enter following the death of a loved one. We may rightfully think of it as being more of a deep chasm or a bottomless pit, with inescapable walls. These valleys are difficult to tolerate and escape, but reaching out to God's lovingly extended hand allows us to heal and understand!

> *"Blessed are those who mourn,*
> *for they shall be comforted."*
> *—Matthew 5:4*

I personally experienced my own first valley of grief just prior to my sixth birthday. My precious father, whom I loved so very deeply, died a painful death at age 49. (This word – love – so inadequately describes what I felt for my father. This feeling defies being put into human words.)

After learning of his death, a sickening, longing loneliness that no tears or any amount of sympathy could satisfy had completely enveloped me. The hollow emptiness that I felt could never be filled by another accompanied me day and night.

But I soon learned that if I could slip away unnoticed, I could run to a small stream of water that coursed its way through the farm property we had rented. There, the stream was lined with multiple large towering, beckoning trees, bearing sturdy limbs and an abundance of rustling green leaves. Here, hidden from the rest of the world, I found the healing power of God's nature as I climbed as high as I could and lay among the inviting branches. Birds sang their comforting laments to me as I cried and as I talked to God about my grief from which I knew only He could help me recover. I visited there as often as I could get away until I was finally able to face the world without tears of grief at every thought of my father's untimely death.

The gold nuggets I found in this valley as I matured were that God had lovingly helped me replace my bitter anguish and sorrow with more love for, and trust in, Him: and had replaced the sadness with the true abiding joy that only He Himself can provide. The cost of this abiding joy? The blood of Jesus Christ, our Savior. Everlasting, thankful praise be to God for His love for us in providing this cleansing sacrifice!

After the death of a loved one, we may grieve because of something we said or something we feel we should have done or done differently for the deceased. Perhaps we didn't interact with them enough; perhaps caught up in our problems, we overlooked their problems; perhaps we raised our voice to them when we should have been caring and supportive. God tells us if we spend our time looking back, we are unproductive. Instead, we can repent, if necessary, and be forgiven if we have sinned. Will that gold we mined from this time of sorrow reveal to us that we need to be more compassionate and caring, more loving, more patient, more tolerant, more attentive, and less judgmental or domineering in the future? Here we can apply the Golden Rule: "Do unto others as you would have them do unto you." Parents or grandparents do not become our children as we care for them. God instructs us to honor their age.

These are valuable learning nuggets for our continued growth as servants of God. Ridding our hearts of revealed inadequacies can only, without fail, produce better, more loving, and kind servants of God.

"He is on the path of life who heeds instruction,
But he who ignores reproof goes astray."
—Proverbs 10:17

25

"Blessed are the pure in heart, for they shall see God."
—Matthew 5:8

ॐ

God's Plans

Dear Lord, if we think we can't survive
Without some "loved one" in our lives,
Please be so kind as to help us see,
We cannot plan our lives, but Thee.

Help us to take your kind advice,
To let your peace dwell in our lives,
As we embrace the trials we fear,
And live with joy, because you're near.

Our bodies have never been ours, but Thine:
We live on this earth by "Your" design.
May each day of our lives, a sacrifice be,
As we forfeit our plans, to live for Thee.
Amen!

ॐ

"Since his days are determined,
the number of his months is with You;
And his limits You have set so that he cannot pass."
—Job 14:5

This is not to suggest that God does not listen to our prayers, as the account of Hezekiah, the king, tells us that God added fifteen years to his life when he prayed to Him. "Before Isaiah had gone out of the middle court, the word of the Lord came to him, saying, 'Return and say to Hezekiah the leader of My people, 'Thus says the Lord, the God of your father David, 'I have heard your prayer, I have seen your tears; behold, I will heal you. On the third day you shall go up to the house of the Lord. I will add fifteen years to your life, and I will deliver you and this city from the hand of the King of Assyria; and I will defend this city for My own sake and for My servant David's sake'" (2 Kings 20:4-6).

Sadly, we may find ourselves in a regret-filled "self-made pit" because of the sin(s) we have committed, with sorrow and guilt burdening us. Carelessly, we have allowed ourselves to become a pawn of Satan. *"For our struggle is not against flesh and blood, but against the rulers, against the powers, against the world forces of this darkness, against the spiritual forces of wickedness in the heavenly places" (Ephesians 6:12)*. So, I should ask myself: have I left this kind of darkness behind, or am I still wallowing in the soul-condemning wickedness of Satan's despicable valleys?

If we allow Satan to plant emotions of distrust, hate, lust, greed, or pride in our hearts while in a valley, we will be unable to escape it without first seeking God's help and forgiveness. One man who was successful in escaping his self-made valley by repenting and confessing his sins of adultery and murder: King David's penitent heart and his love for God and His statutes allowed him to overcome his sin and escape to become a favored and profitable servant of God (2 Samuel 11:1-12:25). Even though he escaped, he still had to deal with his painful memories:

> *"For I know my transgressions,*
> *and my sin is ever before me."*
> —Psalm 51:3

And so it is with us; our sins of darkness, against our perfect God who is light, are always remembered with deep, shameful, and sorrowful regret. Those who have followed God's plan to become His children can find forgiveness by repenting, praying for forgiveness, and turning from sin; But just as King David learned, our sins cannot be completely erased from our minds.

Thus, we must continue to reach upward to God (as we mine our pit), who reassures us of His love and His flawless forgiving grace.

> *"Therefore humble yourselves*
> *under the mighty hand of God,*
> *that He may exalt you at the proper time."*
> —1 Peter 5:6

&

"He will not always strive with us,
Nor will He keep His anger forever.
He has not dealt with us according to our sins,
Nor rewarded us according to our iniquities.
For as high as the heavens are above the earth, so great is
His lovingkindness toward those who fear Him.

As far as the east is from the west,
So far has He removed our transgressions from us."
—Psalm 103:9-12

ॐ

"Who is a God like You, who pardons iniquity
And passes over the rebellious act of the remnant
of His possession? He does not retain His anger forever,
Because He delights in unchanging love."
—Micah 7:18

He is our God of great mercy and loving grace! May we continuingly let our gratitude be made known to Him!

Again, as we remember King David, we will recall God allowed David's son to die as a consequence of his father's sins (2 Samuel 12:14). In this account, a valuable gold nugget is that David believed he knew his baby's destination and that he could live a Godly life and finally be with him throughout eternity (2 Samuel 12:23).

Unlike David, there are those whose hearts are so hardened, perhaps because of greed, that fall prey to sin that may ultimately destroy them. Judas, one of the twelve apostles, selfishly betrayed Jesus the Christ (who loved him) for ONLY thirty pieces of silver. He later ended his own life due to regret and shame that came too late (Acts 1:15-18).

We must be very careful that we do not allow our own regret and shame to come too late!

From these examples, we can be sure that any sin left in our lives will place our souls in a "condemned" state that will remain until we consult and act on God's gracious plan for forgiveness.

"For You, Lord, are good, and ready to forgive,
And abundant in lovingkindness to all who call upon You."
—Psalm 86:5

And now may we continue to gain endurance from a journal entry by David Ditter, dated 8/3/2015:

> "We were privileged to, once again, gather together as the body of the only begotten Son of God and proclaim his death until he returns. So thankful to be reminded, once again of the promises of God toward those that love him and how bountifully God blesses his children that wait on him. We were strengthened to continue to travel the strait path and to glorify and praise the name of the Holy One of Israel. Rhonda felt very good all day and proclaimed her thankfulness to do so. She was also able to sleep most of the late afternoon and early evening. Her appetite remains strong and healthy and she manages her pain very well these days. Thanks be to God for you all and for His care."
>
> (Rhonda's cancer was first diagnosed August 16, 2012. Their lives remained focused on Godly perseverance, even until her departure. May we find God's comfort in their examples of faithful service.)

"The Lord is my light and my salvation; Whom shall I fear?
The Lord is the defense of my life; Whom shall I dread?"
—Psalm 27:1

Sunsets

It is God who provides breathtaking sunsets,
A show of rare beauty, for you and for me.
His paintbrush He fills with bright colors,
Gorgeous hues, for the whole world to see!

But it is only me, who colors my sunset,
I decide what its colors will be.
If I paint with the black or the gray ones,
They will be what the world will see.

Today, as we walk toward our sunset,
If we find dark colors therein,
Repentance and prayers for forgiveness,
Can cleanse God's children's souls of all sin.

May our sunsets be colored so brightly,
Other souls may also want to win.
And when we meet God at our sunset,
He will be there to welcome us in!

(Dedicated to Nel Hazelwood, who makes
it a daily priority to reflect the beauty of
rainbows into the lives of others.)

ℰꙨ

"As the hand is made for holding and the eye for seeing,
You have fashioned me for joy.
Share with me the vision that shall find it everywhere:
In the wild violet's beauty,
In the lark's melody,
In the face of a steadfast man,
In a child's smile,
In a mother's love,
In the purity of Jesus."
—A Gaelic Prayer

Chapter 2

Preparing Our Minds and Souls
for Future Valleys

When God created man, He placed a longing for His Creator in his heart and a deep need to be able to lean wholly on Him to obtain His infinite wisdom and grace; thus, to enjoy the prospect and gift of eternal life with Him. This was an act of lovingkindness on God's part; He is perfect in His love for mankind. Who then, but our Creator, can fully discern our needs; what is right and good for us? It then follows He must require an "obedient" faith: a commitment to living and doing all things according to His perfect will.

> If you are presently living in rebellion to God, understand that God wants you to repent. But know also that God is not going to compel or force you in any way to do his will. Yes, our God moves in a mysterious way, and he will discipline and help to guide you to the right path, but he will not force the issue. To make you obey would rob God of what he desires most...your love." —David Maxson

Here, for those seeking the stability, shelter, and comfort the Savior offers, you will find the following scriptures reveal God's plan of salvation. This plan is not according to man's will, but according to God's "own" perfect will.

> *"And do not be conformed to this world,*
> *but be transformed by the renewing of*
> *your mind, so that you may prove what*
> *the will of God is, that which is good and*
> *acceptable and perfect."*
> *—Romans 12:2*

As His revealed will is *perfect*, it is complete in every way, without flaw or fault of any kind.

"Not everyone who says to Me, 'Lord, Lord,'
will enter the kingdom of heaven,
but he who does the will of My Father
who is in heaven will enter."
—Matthew 7:21

ℬ

"When we try to "go it alone," the result is bound to be either discouragement on the one hand, or pride on the other. If we fail to be comforted by the availability of God's grace, we bog down in despair. But if we fail to be humbled by the necessity of God's guidance and help, we bog down in something even worse: the illusion that we're doing better than we really are." –Gary Henry

ℬ

Hear, then, the invitation of Jesus:
"Come to Me, all who are weary and heavy-laden,
and I will give you rest. Take My yoke upon you and
learn from Me, for I am gentle and humble in heart,
and YOU WILL FIND REST FOR YOUR SOULS.
For My yoke is easy and My burden is light."
—Matthew 11:28-30

And now, to obtain and secure an obedient, persevering faith, God has provided adequately for us: *"So faith comes from hearing, and hearing by the word of Christ" (Romans 10:17).* The following conversation took place after Christ's resurrection: *"When they saw Him, they worshiped Him; but some were doubtful. And Jesus came up and spoke to them, saying, "All authority has been given to Me in heaven and on earth"* (Matt 28:17-18). This scripture gives us confidence we can safely use His commands as our blueprint to obtain our goal of heaven. He has ALL authority here and in heaven.

And from Him, we learn the following:

"And He was saying to them,
"You are from below, I am from above;
you are of this world, I am not of this world.
Therefore I said to you that you will die in your sins;
for unless you believe that I am He,
you will die in your sins."
—John 8:23-24

"Therefore everyone who confesses Me before men, I will also confess him before My Father who is in heaven. But whoever denies Me before men, I will also deny him before My Father who is in heaven" (Matthew 10:32-33). Here, Jesus is teaching us, after believing, we must confess Him as our Lord and Savior.

"From that time Jesus began to preach and say,
"Repent, for the kingdom of heaven is at hand."
—Matthew 4:17

Repentance (Godly sorrow for our sins) is also a necessary step in every true conversion.

"And He said to them,
"Go into all the world and preach
the gospel to all creation.
He who has believed and has
been baptized shall be saved;
but he who has disbelieved
shall be condemned."
—Mark 16:15-16

Baptism is a command and is not left for our discrimination. It is a necessary part of the gospel Jesus commanded His apostles to preach, and disobedience to that command Jesus labels as "disbelief." Baptism is not a symbolic step in salvation but a necessary "burial" in water.

Peter witnessed many miracles performed by Jesus, the transfiguration, and the crucifixion of Christ. Additionally, having been with Him after His resurrection, was qualified to testify: *"Therefore let all the house of Israel know for certain that God has made Him both Lord and Christ—*

this Jesus whom you crucified." Now when they heard this, they were pierced to the heart, and said to Peter and the rest of the apostles, "Brethren, what shall we do?" Peter said to them, "Repent, and each of you be baptized in the name of Jesus Christ for the forgiveness of your sins; and you will receive the gift of the Holy Spirit. For the promise is for you and your children and for all who are far off, as many as the Lord our God will call to Himself" (Acts 2:36-39).

"For you are all sons of God through faith in Christ Jesus.
For all of you who were baptized into Christ have clothed
yourselves with Christ. There is neither Jew nor Greek,
there is neither slave nor free man, there is neither male
nor female; for you are all one in Christ Jesus. And if you
belong to Christ, then you are Abraham's descendants,
heirs according to promise."
—Galatians 3:26-29

℘

"Therefore I, the prisoner of the Lord,
implore you to walk in a manner worthy of the calling
with which you have been called,
with all humility and gentleness,
with patience, showing tolerance for one another in love,
being diligent to preserve the unity of the Spirit
in the bond of peace.
There is one body and one Spirit,
just as also you were called in one hope of your calling;
one Lord, one faith, one baptism,
one God and Father of all,
who is over all and through all and in all."
—Ephesians 4:1-6

What a beautiful, unifying passage. His church is to be "one" in faith and obedience to His commands. Let us note who is imploring us to pay attention to this unifying gold nugget of scripture—Paul, who is now in prison for preaching the saving truth of the gospel; the apostle chosen by the Lord on his way to Damascus to imprison believers in Christ (Acts 9:1-17). It was on that road the Lord told him he would show him how much he would suffer for His name's sake. Paul courageously accepted the Lord's call to work! Even at this time, while in prison, he remains zealous for His God! Who could possibly be better qualified to "implore" us to be united in "one hope of your calling"?

"He is before all things,
and in Him all things hold together.
He is also head of the body, the church;
and He is the beginning,
the firstborn from the dead, so that He Himself
will come to have first place in everything."
—Colossians 1:17-18

The Holy Spirit revealed this pattern of complete obedience: therefore, it is not to be changed by any man or even an angel from heaven. *"All Scripture is inspired by God and profitable for teaching, for reproof, for correction, for training in righteousness; so that the man of God may be adequate, equipped for every good work"* (2 Timothy 3:16-17).

"But even if we, or an angel from heaven,
should preach to you a gospel contrary to
what we have preached to you,
he is to be accursed!"
—Galatians 1:8

ॐ

"I testify to everyone who hears the words of the
prophecy of this book: if anyone adds to them,
God will add to him the plagues
which are written in this book;
and if anyone takes away from the words of the
book of this prophecy, God will take away his part from
the tree of life and from the holy city,
which are written in this book."
—Revelation 22:18-19

Note: Jesus, our example, was baptized. Not for the remission of sins as He was sinless, but it was to fulfill all righteousness as He pleased His Father (John 8:29). And please Him, He did! *"Then Jesus arrived from Galilee at the Jordan coming to John, to be baptized by him. But John tried to prevent Him saying, 'I have need to be baptized by You, and do You come to me?' But Jesus answering said to Him, 'Permit it at this time; for in this way it is fitting for us to fulfill all righteousness.' Then he permitted Him. After being baptized, Jesus came up immediately from the water; and behold, the heavens were opened, and he saw the Spirit of God descending as a dove and lighting on Him, and behold, a voice out of the heavens said, 'This is My beloved Son, in whom I am well-pleased'"* (Matthew 3:13-17).

There is no sprinkling or pouring here. Jesus came up from the water, pleasing His Father. We see the same kind of immersion when Philip baptized the Eunuch (Acts 8:27-39). Any other method defies Jesus' authority and example.

Before becoming obedient followers of Christ, we lacked access to God to help us through our earthly valleys; but now, in Christ, we have the blessed privilege of prayer. Through repentance and prayer, we can ask for and receive forgiveness of sin. Also included in this "grace package" is the ability to seek wisdom through prayer and the peace that comes from and with a right relationship with God.

> *"Now to Him who is able to do far more abundantly*
> *beyond all that we ask or think,*
> *according to the power that works within us, to Him*
> *be the glory in the church and in Christ Jesus to all*
> *generations forever and ever. Amen."*
> —Ephesians 3:20-21

Remembering my baptism: I was 13 years old and had realized earlier that I had sinned and was in immediate need of being cleansed in the waters of baptism as Christ directs. However, at that time, my mother thought I needed to wait until I was older before taking on the responsibility of serving God. That period of waiting to do what I knew was right was filled with anxiety and a dark dread that I might die while still living in sin. But now that my mother had finally agreed, both my brother, eleven months older, and I confessed Christ as our Savior.

We were living on a farm in Kansas. The weather was bitter cold, and ice covered the water in my uncle's cement "cattle watering" tank. In addition to providing water for his cows, it was also used as a baptistry when needed. Inwardly I was grateful for the cold weather and the ice since the water in the tank was looking stale and completely uninviting.

36

Instead, we drove to the Wellington church building where there was a warm baptistry. I could hardly wait to confess Christ and step into the water in grateful obedience that would finally wash away my condemning sins. Coming up out of that watery grave, I felt the weight of sin lifted, and instead felt pure and clean, clothed in the loving grace of God. This was the most joyful, powerful, and uplifting experience I have ever known or will ever know again while on this earth.

I am indebted to my parents, my Bible class teacher, and to my uncle David and Aunt Bettie (who so lovingly cared for me during the multiple times my father was in the hospital) for instilling in my heart a love for God and the urgent desire to serve Him. May God be forever praised!

Being obedient followers of Christ better prepares us to mine future valleys, and our hearts will yearn to tell others about God's eternal plan of salvation, His gift that saves us from spiritual death and eternal punishment.

"Be diligent to present yourself approved to God
as a workman who does not need to be ashamed,
accurately handling the word of truth."
—2 Timothy 2:15

ଔ

"Be devoted to one another in brotherly love;
give preference to one another in honor,
not lagging behind in diligence, fervent in spirit,
serving the Lord; rejoicing in hope, persevering in tribulation,
devoted to prayer, contributing to the needs of the saints,
practicing hospitality."
—Romans 12:10-13

Setting goals: after our conversion, goals are an important step toward spiritual growth and success so that we can correctly handle and be obedient to the "word of truth." Simply setting those goals does not cause action by itself, but "self-control" (discipline) causes us to do what we would otherwise neglect. Our goals should include time for daily Bible study, quiet time for prayer, reaching out to the sick, those lost in sin, and those discouraged, calling or sending cards to those who need our encouragement. This kind of goal setting will not allow us to become lax in doing what we can do, even as we mature in years. Older men and women may have to master the temptation to neglect doing what they are still capable of accomplishing. God does not mention retiring from serving Him. If the apostles had taken this attitude, a great multitude of souls, who were the very necessary foundation of the church, would have been eternally lost because of it. God's perfect plan was at work, even to the end of their lives!

"Whatever your hand finds to do, do it with all your might;
for there is no activity or planning or knowledge or wisdom
in Sheol (the grave) where you are going."
—Ecclesiastes 9:10

Perhaps this is an opportune time to evaluate our remaining God-given talents! May we consider what an honor it is to serve our all-powerful, all-knowing God!

"I press on toward the goal for the prize of the
upward call of God in Christ Jesus."
—Philippians 3:14

I wish I had always followed my goals more perfectly. In doing so, I would have escaped some of the painful valleys necessary to teach me what I had neglected to learn or accept at a younger age. I thank God for His patience in teaching me through those deep, agonizingly painful valleys that clearly revealed things I needed to change in my life. Sometimes the valleys were such that they became very distracting, and I allowed them to swallow my time without mining for gold in the scriptures or thanking God for His blessings as much as I should. This kind of self-centered day became a day of spiritual emptiness, ending in a feeling of remorse for having cheated myself. God needs nothing from me. He merely desires my love and obedience, but I am dependent on Him for every aspect of my physical and spiritual existence: our ever-present God!

"The greater danger for most of us is not
that our aim (goal) is too high and we miss it,
but that it is too low, and we reach it."
—Author unknown

Further counsel from God reminds us that eliminating anxiety from our lives contributes to happier, healthier lives.

"Anxiety in a man's heart weighs it down,
But a good word makes it glad."
—Proverbs 12:25

ℰℐ

"Rejoice in the Lord always; again I will say, rejoice!
Let your gentle spirit be known to all men.
The Lord is near.
Be anxious for nothing, but in everything
by prayer and supplication with thanksgiving
let your requests be made known to God.
And the peace of God, which surpasses
all comprehension, will guard your
hearts and your minds in Christ Jesus."
—Philippians 4:4-7

ℰℐ

"Blessed be the Lord, who daily bears our burden,
The God who is our salvation. Selah."
—Psalm 68:19

If I allow anxiety to burden me, I will be ill-prepared to cope with my problems or comfort others who need a brother or sister to help them through their time of stress. And if I am allowing myself to remain stressed, am I not displaying a tarnished image of trust in God?

In preparation for their future to remain strong in the Lord, Christians have the availability of the armor of God. *"Finally, be strong in the Lord and in the strength of His might. Put on the full armor of God, so that you will be able to stand firm against the schemes of the devil. For our struggle is not against flesh and blood, but against the rulers, against the powers, against the world forces of this darkness, against the spiritual forces of wickedness in the heavenly places. Therefore, take up the full armor of God, so that you will be able to resist in the evil day, and having done everything, to stand firm. Stand firm therefore, HAVING GIRDED YOUR LOINS WITH TRUTH, and HAVING PUT ON THE*

39

BREASTPLATE OF RIGHTEOUSNESS, and having shod YOUR FEET WITH THE PREPARATION OF THE GOSPEL OF PEACE; in addition to all, taking up the shield of faith with which you will be able to extinguish all the flaming arrows of the evil one. And take THE HELMET OF SAL-VATION, and the sword of the Spirit, which is the word of God. With all prayer and petition pray at all times in the Spirit, and with this in view, be on the alert with all perseverance and petition for all the saints" (Ephesians 6:10-18).

This scripture makes us aware of the importance of spiritual strength and growth to enable us to stand firm when days of evil come. Am I living a "righteous" life? Am I "fitted with readiness" that comes from the "Gospel of peace?" Am I carrying the "shield of faith" that caused me to become a follower of Christ and thus assures the hearer I am trustworthy of their confidence? Am I prepared and capable of being loving and kind, but firm in God's teachings and expectations, not wavering if others need to lovingly hear how they need to grow, even while in their valleys? Am I using the privilege of "prayer for all the saints" (v. 18) to its fullest extent, for myself and rulers, etc.? Do I view prayer as a burden or as the gracious gift of love and peace that it is? There are times in our lives when we do not even know for what we ought to pray. During this time: *"In the same way the Spirit also helps our weakness; for we do not know how to pray as we should, but the Spirit Himself intercedes for us with groanings too deep for words; and He who searches the hearts knows what the mind of the Spirit is, because He intercedes for the saints according to the will of God"* (Romans 8:26-27). Yet, can we even begin to fully fathom the comfort God's Holy Spirit provides for us? Too, can we even begin to appreciate how the Godhead works as one, always aware of, and working together to fulfill our spiritual needs? Therein lies our strength, our hope, our peace, and our salvation.

God has covered all our bases for us to win in this rugged game of life, but we must allow Him to be our Manager. We must make sure we are not expecting Him to walk with us; but rather that we are walking safely, joyfully, and gratefully with Him.

"Father, you are the giver of every good and perfect gift. We're living in a land flowing with milk and honey, dwelling in homes we didn't build, eating from vineyards we didn't plant, and drinking from wells we didn't dig. Help us to remember that only in Jesus can we find all of these things we don't deserve. Accept our tribute of praise and help us to honor your love through our submissive obedience to your will." —David Maxson

ℰℂ

"By this we know that we have come to know Him, if we keep His commandments."
—1 John 2:3

Another trusting, persevering journal entry by David Ditter, dated 10/3/2015:

"Rhonda slept good last night and arose at a decent hour of the morning. She did a few things around the house, but, for the most part, took it pretty easy today, resting a lot. Her appetite is good, but her energy level was not where she prefers. We were able to reschedule Rhonda's chemo treatments, beginning once more on Monday at ten. We will resume the same schedule as before: Monday, Tuesday, Wednesday and probably followed by granix shots Thursday and Friday. That would be repeated every three weeks. Of course, Rhonda is not enthused about resuming the treatments, but is willing and does still desire to continue the campaign. We look to God for the strength to continue and the wisdom to allow Him to direct our path. We know He has provided all of you to provide the strength, for which we glorify His name, because of your love for Him."

ℰℂ

"By faith Moses, when he had grown up,
refused to be called the son of Pharaoh's daughter,
choosing rather to endure ill-treatment with the people of God
than to enjoy the passing pleasures of sin,
considering the reproach of Christ greater riches
than the treasures of Egypt; for he was looking to the reward.
By faith he left Egypt, not fearing the wrath of the king;
for he endured, as seeing Him who is unseen."
—Hebrews 11:24-27

Chapter 3

Mining for Nuggets of Gold in Job's Excruciating Valley

In the book of Job, God in His unerring wisdom provides an example of a man of unwavering spiritual faithfulness. His example allows us to learn more about perseverance to escape our valleys without asking "why" we are there. After escaping, we can instead ask ourselves what we have learned from this test. As we have already learned, every valley can become a valuable spiritual teacher if we allow it. Job's valley was not an exception to his maturing in the knowledge of God.

Here, God has provided us to take a closer look into some of Satan's valleys used to test Job. They are of such great magnitude that we seldom find their equal elsewhere in the Bible. This man, who was blameless and upright in God's sight, was allowed at the devil's request (1:6-12), to become an object of extreme ridicule and inescapable, prolonged human suffering (Job 1:1 through chapter 36).

Job's question is "why" this should be happening to him when he has been feeling spiritually safe, secure, and pleasing to God. The Holy Spirit makes it abundantly clear, and as we have learned in other chapters, good people will suffer in this life without always knowing why. God spiritually blesses us to be able to look to the end of Job's suffering to see just how God greatly rewarded his perseverance, love, and unwavering respect for God.

> *"We count those blessed who endured.*
> *You have heard of the endurance of Job*
> *and have seen the outcome of the Lord's*
> *dealings, that the Lord is full of compassion*
> *and is merciful."*
> *—James 5:11*

If we, too, wish to be blessed in our perseverance in overcoming our valleys, we have come to the right book to learn more about how to succeed. Here, God clearly reveals His expectation of us is that we will serve Him faithfully in every circumstance without ever permanently falling into Satan's alluring clutches.

When carefully studied, we can see more vividly how God works at times, and yet perhaps not fully understand all the questions the book of Job presents. However, our responsibility is to learn from what the Holy Spirit reveals in this study but leave the hidden things to God. Here, and in other passages in the Bible, God provides some added insight that lets us understand there is more to His realm than we can see or even vaguely begin to imagine OR to comprehend. In the following passages, God permits us to get a small glimpse of that realm: *"And of the angels He says, "WHO MAKES HIS ANGELS WINDS, AND HIS MINISTERS A FLAME OF FIRE" (Hebrews 1:7). "Are they not all ministering spirits, sent out to render service for the sake of those who will inherit salvation"* (Hebrews 1:14)? *"For I am convinced that neither death, nor life, nor angels, nor principalities, nor things present, nor things to come, nor powers, nor height, nor depth, nor any other created thing, will be able to separate us from the love of God, which is in Christ Jesus our Lord"* (Romans 8:38-39). In this last passage, He lovingly leads us to understand we are spiritually secure if we live faithfully, according to His plan for us.

Some of the valuable lessons the book of Job can teach us include how to handle our valleys and how to escape falling into some of them.

> *"Wise men store up knowledge, But with the mouth of the foolish, ruin is at hand."*
> —Proverbs 10:14

It is clear (chapter 1:1) the Holy Spirit wants us to understand, first, that Job was blameless and upright and that he "feared" God. The gold nugget here is that I, too, should fear Him, as Job did, and to fear what He can bring about, or allows Satan to bring about. *"If you address as Father the One who impartially judges according to each one's work, conduct yourselves in fear during the time of your stay on earth"* (1 Peter 1:17). Fearing God will encourage us to persevere in living righteously, knowing our most valuable asset, "our salvation," is at stake. *"The fear of the Lord is to hate evil"* (Proverbs 8:13a). *"And he said with a loud voice, 'Fear God, and give Him glory, because the hour of His judgment has come; worship Him who made the heaven and the earth and sea and springs of waters'"* (Revelation 14:7). In these passages, the fear of God and His love are united.

Job turned away from ("shunned," NIV) evil. How many deep, dark valleys can I escape if I faithfully follow this example?

He was abundantly rich in earthly wealth, and he was "the greatest of all the men of the east" (1:3b). Yet we see he was not conceited or earthly minded, but rather chose to be humble and spiritually rich! *"Instruct those who are rich in this present world not to be conceited or to fix their hope on the uncertainty of riches, but on God, who richly supplies us with all things to enjoy" (1 Timothy 6:17).*

He also very wisely chose to accept living according to the knowledge God had given him. Today we have access to the complete revelation of God to guide us in our service. How very blessed we are to be able to "immerse" ourselves in His wisdom. We do not know what wisdom of God was revealed to Job, but His mind was "on" God! For us, what can be our excuse for not diligently searching His Word and serving Him according to His teaching?

Job was a loving father, motivating him to be deeply interested in the spiritual welfare of his children, sacrificing for them when he thought their souls might be in peril. And he did this continuously (1:5)! (At that time in history, as a patriarch, he would have been head of his house and would have acted as priest for his family).

God's admonition to children and fathers today, is this: *"Children, obey your parents in the Lord, for this is right. HONOR YOUR FATHER AND MOTHER (which is the first commandment with a promise), SO THAT IT MAY BE WELL WITH YOU, AND THAT YOU MAY LIVE LONG ON THE EARTH. Fathers, do not provoke your children to anger, but bring them up in the discipline and instruction of the Lord" (Ephesians 6:1- 4).* (Emphasis mine.)

Here we see God clearly giving an assignment to children and their fathers: and fathers faithfully heeding this admonition will teach their children loving obedience. In doing this they will more clearly understand the value and importance of serving God obediently, even as adults. .

Fathers can also counsel their sons and daughters to choose wisely throughout their lives so they can avoid many of the precarious pitfalls the devil cunningly places in their way. A seemingly often overlooked but necessary aspect of teaching is the importance of dressing modestly; and also, not allowing their bodies to be violated. And of equal importance, teaching them to avoid violating the bodies of others. If overlooked, this could permanently mar their future. Surely, nothing could be more important! Not occupations, television, sports, computer games, love of money, the internet, working out, or any such worldly fatherly pursuits. All the above pale in comparison to the importance of this "God assigned" duty directed to fathers.

The following passages were written to the Israelites: *"Now this is the commandment, the statutes and the judgments which the Lord your God has commanded me to teach you, that you might do them in the land where you are going over to possess it, so that you and your son and your grandson might fear the Lord your God, to keep all His statutes and His commandments which I commanded you, all the days of your life, and that your days may be prolonged"* (Deuteronomy 6:1-2). *"These words, which I am commanding you today, shall be on your heart. You shall teach them diligently to your sons and shall talk of them when you sit in your house and when you walk by the way and when you lie down and when you rise up. You shall bind them as a sign on your hand and they shall be as frontals on your forehead. You shall write them on the doorposts of your house and on your gates"* (Deuteronomy 6:6-9). These timeless passages help us understand how important the commands of God have always been concerning carefully teaching our children with unfailing patience and passion concerning obedience to Him. Does this sound like what we are doing today? Has teaching our children about God become any less important? Not so!

Mothers and even grandmothers: this is a golden opportunity for us also. "For I am mindful of the sincere faith within you, which first dwelt in your grandmother Lois and your mother Eunice, and I am sure that it is in you as well" (2 Timothy 1:5). What did the grandmother and mother gain from teaching Timothy? They gained a grandson, and a son, who became a spiritual giant, who lovingly risked his own life to bring lost souls to Christ. Paul chose him to accompany him on his second missionary journey because he was "well-spoken of by the brethren" (Acts 16:1-3). What a fulfilling, priceless reward! Am I overlooking or neglecting such an opportunity: the opportunity to teach my children or grandchildren so their lives and their accurate teaching of God's word may help save lost souls from punishment? If not, my own soul is in danger.

Women can also assist fathers in teaching daughters concerning modesty: not only with our counsel but also by example in how we dress. Are we showing cleavage? I may need to bend over to check this out. Is my dress too short, too gaudy, too tight? Would we like to see our daughter leave with her date dressed in this fashion? This kind of dress may appear to her date as an open invitation to look or explore further. We can ask ourselves if we are dressed as we would want to be when Jesus returns. Do the words "modestly" and "discreet" describe what I am wearing? Keeping up with fashion is not an assignment from God, nor is popularity. And, we can be sure any immodest allurement is from the devil. I recently read a book about a man who led an extremely sinful life of drugs, alcohol, and unfaithfulness to his faithful wife. He recorded that a woman with bare feet and painted toenails was a lustful attraction to him. A simple thing, but a consideration, nonetheless.

Following are statements from men that should help us with our decisions in our dressing to please God and to avoid tempting men.

"So what does your dress
say about your heart?
Is your heart constrained
by modesty and self-control?
Does your wardrobe reflect a desire
to glorify self or God?
Are you professing worldliness
by your dress, or godliness?"
—David Maxson

"In a world where camisoles are worn as outerwear, the subjects of modesty, propriety, shame-fastness, discretion and chastity all sound kind of old-fashioned. Many have forgotten that the original and primary function of clothing was to cover one's nakedness (Gen 3:7-11, 21), not to accentuate it. Yet much of the clothing produced, pushed, and purchased for public viewing is designed to emphasize, enhance, and increase one's sex appeal. Conversely, the modestly adorned

47

woman communicates meekness, respect, and good works (1 Tim. 2:9-10; 1 Pet. 3:2-4) and will be noticed and appreciated by honorable men. Your brothers would appreciate the help in the battle between the flesh and the spirit"

—Andy Diestelkamp,
a preacher of the Gospel

It is also good when a father leads in grooming his children to be the pillars of the church of tomorrow. Because he is to do this, it then becomes his obligation (and opportunity) to train his children to become godly students; and the girls to be teachers, obedient wives, and loving mothers; and for the boys to be godly husbands, fathers, capable song leaders, future deacons, teachers, elders or preachers. If not, who or what will be responsible for fulfilling that obligation? Their mothers alone, or their Bible class teachers? The television? Or their smartphones?

"It is by his deeds that a lad distinguishes himself
If his conduct is pure and right."
—Proverbs 20:11

Too often overlooked, the word "can't" can hinder children from doing what they can do until someone helps them recognize their God-given talents: and, until they recognize them, they are useless. This is a good opportunity for parents to utilize to help enlighten and encourage their children.

A study conducted in Switzerland confirms the irreplaceable value of fathers in the family concerning teaching their children the value of attending worship services:

"In 1994, the Swiss carried out an extra survey that the researchers for our masters in Europe (I write from England) were happy to record. The question was asked to determine whether a person's religion carried through to the next generation, and if so, why, or if not, why not. The result is dynamite. There is one critical factor. It is overwhelming, and it is this: It is the religious practice of the father of the family that, above all, determines the future attendance at or absence from church of the children." —Robbie Low, The Truth About Fathers and The Church

Professor Paul Vitz's book, *Faith of the Fatherless*, recorded that many of the most notorious of atheist philosophers had a poor relationship with their earthly fathers. This should deeply touch every father's heart! But as for Job, spiritual matters were first in his life (he rose up to sacrifice early in the morning). This was his regular custom after his adult children had finished feasting (1:5). Do we also feel the urgent need for setting this kind of "family" priority in our lives? If not, we can add this valuable nugget of placing God "first" in our children's lives to our collection gleaned from God's revealed account of this faithful and beloved servant.

We now see God setting the limits for Satan to test Job's loyalty to Him (1:6-2:6). And for us: *"No temptation has overtaken you but such as is common to man; and God is faithful, who will not allow you to be tempted beyond what you are able, but with the temptation will provide the way of escape also, so that you will be able to endure it"* (1 Corinthians 10:13). God's love, assurance, and protection are always at work for us! God knew Job's limits, and He knows ours as well, but I must "look" for the way of escape when I am tempted.

Alarmingly, Satan was allowed to use powers in his testing of Job that are only under God's control. *"The fire of God fell from heaven"* (1:16b), *"a great wind came from across the wilderness"* (1:19a). An awesome and fearful revelation! Satan allowed to use God's power? The gold nugget in this is that Satan can only use the power God allows him to have.

Job's ten children and all that he owned had been completely wiped out of his life, *"Then Job arose and tore his robe and shaved his head, and fell to the ground and worshiped"* (1:20). *"Through all of this Job did not sin nor did he blame God"* (1:22). There was no loss of integrity, though he was ruined without cause. This is a powerful nugget for us to grasp. This is called unshakable, solid, unwavering TRUST in God! Can our finite minds even begin to comprehend the change this immense loss made in his life? Will I fall to my knees in humble worship when tragedy befalls me, my husband, or my children? OR will I just fall to my knees petitioning God for help? Will anger be my response, replacing worship? And, I can only answer, "I pray for spiritual strength to worship Him on my knees during every trial as I should!"

Job was also without a home. There would be no more early morning sacrifices for his children, or overseeing the care of his livestock. The luxury of sleeping in a bed and waking up refreshed after a good night of rest is in the past. He had no money or ability to do good for others as he was accustomed to doing. Question: "Should I not do more worshiping and less questioning God? And what about feeling sorry for myself because of every little bump in the road?" Perhaps I am extinguishing my spiritual light that should be shining brightly to help others more clearly see the way of salvation. Job's light shines brilliantly, even today and forevermore! Praise Him who has revealed Job's life of loving service to us!

The second chapter of Job leads us to the second level of his continued testing. Satan's taunts to God reveal how selfish and brutal he is and to what lengths he will go to destroy our faith (2:4-5). He is a deceiver and a murderer who wants Job (and us) to fall to his debased, demonic level. He was responsible for the untimely deaths of Job's children, and he is just as capable of causing our physical or spiritual death. He may cunningly bait us with alcohol, drugs, infidelity, or money, and the list is far too long to enumerate.

Satan's challenges to cause Job to sin, to this point, have been unsuccessful; so, his next attempt will cause him unthinkable "very personal physical" suffering and moral degradation. Job describes it as grief weighing more than the sand of the seas (6:2-3) and speaks of "My flesh is clothed with worms and a crust of dirt, My skin hardens and runs" (7:5). Can we fathom this? Job had no place to take a warm shower or pain medication to ease his suffering as we do today! I ask myself how I would have reacted. Would it have been like Satan wanted me to act? Am I allowing myself to be dependent on addictive pain medication? This is a very grave and fearful lesson for me to consider. Perhaps I should pray less for my comfort in trials and suffering and more that I am able to withstand the dangerous taunts, temptations, and persecutions of the destructive evil one. "Be of sober spirit, be on the alert.

50

*Your adversary, the devil, prowls
around like a roaring lion, seeking
someone to devour. But resist him,
firm in your faith, knowing that the
same experiences of suffering are
being accomplished by your brethren
who are in the world."
—1 Peter 5:8-9*

Even yet, we see blameless Job, a disgusting sight in the eyes of men, remain pure and steadfast in the sight of God. Painful boils from the soles of his feet to the crown of his head now cover him, but he wisely avoids Satan's trap (2:7). And he continues to provide God with good reason to have confidence in him; this spiritual giant whose trusting, obedient faith remains sufficient for every painful, debasing testing situation Satan assigns him. Am I mentally examining my own faith?

The Holy Spirit now reveals how Satan uses Job's wife as she succumbs to his plot and withdraws all loyal support from her husband; and further, any reverence for God as she asks, *"Then his wife said to him, 'Do you still hold fast to your integrity? Curse God and die'" (Job 2:9)!* God does not reveal to us what eventually happened to Job's wife. This is not ours to question, but we know without a doubt that her approach is not what God would have ours to be. *"Let no unwholesome word proceed from your mouth, but only such a word as is good for edification according to the need of the moment, so that it will give grace to those who hear" (Ephesians 4:29).* This is a valuable nugget for us to heed to avoid many dark deep valleys. *"If anyone thinks himself to be religious, and yet does not bridle his tongue but deceives his own heart, this man's religion is worthless" (James 1:26).* We see Job very carefully restraining his tongue after this taunt, and throughout this entire book so far as it concerns any degradation of the One he valiantly "trusted" to be the perfect and all-powerful God. And, because of this trust he continues to maintain a persevering triumph over Satan!

Another nugget for our learning in this passage is that our perseverance should not depend in any way on how our mate perseveres. Their spiritual performance, or that of any other person touching our lives, is not an acceptable reason for any weakness or rebellion on our part. Someone has observed that sometimes we allow ourselves to become "addicted" to our parents, friends, or mate, and we think we cannot live without them. We should love them as instructed but not allow them to influence our spirituality. *"Husbands, love your wives, just as Christ also loved the church and gave himself up for her"* (Ephesians 5:25). *"Older women likewise are to be reverent in their behavior, not malicious gossips nor enslaved to much wine, teaching what is good, so that they may encourage the young women to love their husbands, to love their children, to be sensible, pure, workers at home, kind, being subject to their own husbands, so that the word of God will not be dishonored"* (Titus 2:3-5). Are we aware that young women may need to LEARN to love their own husbands and their children? Can we not understand how this could be true if they came from a broken home? Or were raised with an unbelieving father or mother? Does my reverent behavior reflect Christ so that I am capable of teaching them? This scripture puts women in a very responsible position. Dishonor to the word of God may result from our neglecting to fulfill this obligation. Our perseverance is a must in every circumstance, including when our mate refuses to join us in that pursuit.

Job now poses a mind searching and appropriate question: *"But he said to her, 'You speak as one of the foolish women speaks. Shall we indeed accept good from God and not accept adversity?'" In all this Job did not sin with his lips"* (Job 2:10b). Job's example of unwavering dependability fully answers this question for us; "YES"! He did! And we, too, can obediently accept both.

He does not overly lament about what he has lost in the way of earthly possessions. Here is a gold nugget for us to evaluate ourselves. Allowing the loss or lack of earthly possessions to affect my spirituality negatively is to sin.

> *"Do not love the world nor the things in the world.*
> *If anyone loves the world, the love of the*
> *Father is not in him."*
> —1 John 2:15

As we continue to mine Job's valley, we find three of his friends have joined him, weeping, tearing their robes, and sprinkling dust on their heads. They sat on the ground with him for seven days and seven nights (sympathetically; possibly even in their torn robes) without speaking a word to him because of his great suffering (2:11-13). These appear to be the kind of friends that would remain diligently faithful and comforting, even under the very worst circumstances. But it appears Satan is cunningly setting another "testing trap" for Job by using these friends.

Now, Job breaks the silence, crying out for answers. *"Why is light given to a man whose way is hidden, and whom God has hedged in" (3:23)?* But he continues to persevere, waiting for answers from God.

> *"...keep yourselves in the love of God,*
> *waiting anxiously for the mercy*
> *of our Lord Jesus Christ to eternal life."*
> —Jude 21

Chapter 4 follows with those who came to comfort him, who have joined with Satan, first offering praise for what Job has done, but following that with criticism and false, debasing accusations. This is another gold nugget we need to consider when we are offering sympathy. "Do not judge so that you will not be judged. For in the way you judge, you will be judged; and by your standard of measure, it will be measured to you" (Matthew 7:1-2). Jesus is warning us to be very careful about our judgmental attitude toward others, such as Job's friends displayed. Satan will be using us as his pawns if we succumb to this kind of behavior. Consider this instead when offering comfort: "I could strengthen you with my mouth, and the solace of my lips could lessen your pain" (Job 16:5). Our assignment from God is to offer the comfort we know, as Job suggested. "So that He sets on high those who are lowly, and those who mourn are lifted to safety" (5:11). Are we spiritually aware the solace of our lips could lessen someone's pain? Are we using that gift as much as God would have us? Or are we even looking for that opportunity?

As we approach the last chapters of the book, his friends continue to accuse and force Job to defend himself, allowing us to see more clearly what caused the Holy Spirit to record: *"There was a man in the land of Uz whose name was Job; and that man was blameless, upright, fearing God and turning away from evil" (1:1). Through all this Job did not sin nor did he blame God" (1:22).*

In chapter 29:2, Job looks back and, again, takes up the discourse, "Oh that I were as in months gone by, As in the days when God watched over me." Do we have days when we waste our time looking back? Days when we feel God is not watching over us? We know Job was suffering, but we will learn that God WAS continuing to watch over him, just as He watches over us.

Continuing chapter 29:11-17, he laments: *"For when the ear heard, it called me blessed, And when the eye saw, it gave witness of me, Because I delivered the poor who cried for help, And the orphan who had no helper. The blessing of the one ready to perish came upon me, And I made the widow's heart sing for joy. I put on righteousness, and it clothed me; My justice was like a robe and a turban. I was eyes to the blind and feet to the lame. I was a father to the needy, And I investigated the case which I did not know. I broke the jaws of the wicked and snatched the prey from his teeth."* He then contrasts that with his present state in chapter 30:28-31. *"I go about mourning without comfort; I stand up in the assembly and cry out for help. I have become a brother to jackals and a companion of ostriches. My skin turns black on me, and my bones burn with fever. Therefore my harp is turned to mourning, And my flute to the sound of those who weep."* This account causes me to ask myself if there is someone in my life who is crying out for help whom I am neglecting. Perhaps this is a good time to ask ourselves if we could do better things with our time. Having lunch with a friend may be a good thing, but would visiting someone who is ill, grieving, stressed, lonely, spiritually ill, or a babe in Christ be a better servant's choice? Perhaps I could take lunch to a shut-in and stay to eat with them. (Clear the way to do this by asking first.) For a clear answer concerning what my priority should be, we may need to ask ourselves, "What would Jesus have me to do?" I think there might be times He would recommend that we women need to be keepers at home. There is great value in teaching our children to work.

Have we faced the fact that we have absolutely no control over our lives except for the choices (decisions) we make? God is in control unless we give limited power to the devil. May we choose wisely! A choice I make could change the course of someone's life, or even my own!

Chapter 31 begins with the man God allows us to see as blameless and upright. *"I have made a covenant with my eyes; How then could I gaze at a virgin?" And what is the portion of God from above or the heritage of the Almighty from on high?" Is it not calamity to the unjust and disaster to those who work iniquity? "Does He not see my ways and number all my steps"* (1-4)? Failing to follow this example has caused many to fall into Satan's baited trap. Should we not keep this nugget of warning locked deep within our hearts to warn us Satan is alive and well and lurking around every corner! The devil may appear as that cute young girl in tight jeans or a very lovely lady, perhaps in skimpy, revealing clothing that is eye catching or, perhaps, even as someone we thought was our very best friend. Satan may catch any of us in a weak moment, and if we do not have a covenant with our eyes we may easily succumb to his temptations. And yes, a deep, vile valley awaits us filled with "calamity and disaster"! This nugget is more like a warning light flashing continuously! This is Satan in disguise. *"No wonder, for even Satan disguises himself as an angel of light" (2 Corinthians 11:14).*

The remainder of Chapter 31 deals in further defense of his character and his way of life.

"Then the Lord answered Job out of the whirlwind and said, 'Who is this that darkens counsel By words without knowledge'" (38:1-2)? This chapter and through chapter 41 serve to remind him (and us) of God's unfathomable wisdom and unearthly, supernatural power. We, too, are blessed as we are reminded of this every moment we are alive and able to consider the intricacy of our bodies. The snow and rain and the galaxies in His heavens are also visible reminders of His great power. But these passages drive home more of the big picture of what our God has done and can continue to do for and to us. Though His rain and snow have blessed us, we have not seen God's storehouse for them, nor can we tip the water jars of the heavens. This ALMIGHTY God is OUR OWN loving Father, full of grace and mercy, the GREAT I AM! May we worship Him in Spirit and in truth! Jesus declares, "But an hour is coming, and now is, when the true worshipers will worship the Father in spirit and truth; for such people the Father seeks to be His worshipers. God is spirit, and those who worship Him must worship in spirit and truth" (John 4:23-24). We must keep our minds in check during worship service, so we are each one of His true worshipers He seeks. Thinking of what we are having for our lunch hardly fits the description of worship!

This loving chastening from God humbles Job, and he now confesses the sin of speaking of things he did not understand (42:1-6). This nugget reminds us to be very careful to teach others only what we learn and understand from His Holy word. "But as for you, speak the things which are fitting for sound doctrine" (Titus 2:1). Confessing our own sin is the only way to clear our conscience and to be able to ask forgiveness. God is listening and desires for us to be renewed in our relationship with Him.

Job retracts and repents in dust and ashes as he extols his loving Master and casts away his own pride. Job's example of true repentance is an example that guides us to what is acceptable to our Father. I thank God for this example of His grace and forgiveness extended to Job. However, I have to ask myself if I follow Job's example of humbly and sorrowfully repenting when I sin?

Chapter 42 is very clear in proving Job's friends have been part of Satan's failed plan to ruin righteous Job. The Lord was angry with them, required sacrifice for their sins, and Job was to pray for them (42:7-8). Thus, a final ending to Satan's unsuccessful attempt to ruin faithful, trusting, and persevering Job.

These men have now been released from Satan's clutches through repentance, sacrifices, prayer, and the grace of a loving, forgiving God (42:9). Jesus the Christ was and is our spiritual sacrifice. However, like Job, we must also present our bodies as living sacrifices if God will reward us in the end (Romans 12:1-2).

Chapter 42:10-13 gives a full account of his rewards for his faithfulness to his Creator. *"The Lord restored the fortunes of Job when he prayed for his friends, and the Lord increased all that Job had twofold. Then all his brothers and all his sisters and all who had known him before came to him, and they ate bread with him in his house; and they consoled him and comforted him for all the adversities that the Lord had brought on him. And each one gave him one piece of money, and each a ring of gold. The Lord blessed the latter days of Job more than his beginning; and he had 14,000 sheep and 6,000 camels and 1,000 yoke of oxen and 1,000 female donkeys. He had seven sons and three daughters."* (Note that he now has a home as one of his blessings that he lovingly and hospitably opens to his brothers, sisters, and friends. We might be constrained to ask, "Where were they when he needed encouragement?" If so, we need to ask ourselves if we have ever allowed any disloyalty of others to keep us from doing what is right and good.

"After this, Job lived 140 years, and saw his sons and his grandsons, four generations. And Job died, an old man and full of days" (42:16-17).

This was indeed worth persevering to obtain as he now continues to have heaven as the perfect reward!

"The backslider in heart will have his fill of his own ways,
But a good man will be satisfied with his."
—Proverbs 14:14

Now, the final question: what did Job learn from his "valley of suffering and torment" that seemed insurmountable but brought him to a better level of spiritual understanding and growth?

1. Questioning God is never necessary.
2. Bodily suffering can teach and strengthen perseverance.
3. Trusting God is the right thing to do, even when it appears to be futile.
4. Your best friends or even beloved relatives may become Satan's advocates, but forgiveness is available for them after repentance and turning from sin.
5. When we talk about Him, God wants us to know what we are saying is in harmony with His word.
6. We never reach perfection, and continuing to grow spiritually should be a never-ending process.

"And this I pray, that your love may abound
still more and more in real knowledge and all discernment,
so that you may approve the things that are excellent,
in order to be sincere and blameless until the day of Christ;
having been filled with the fruit of righteousness
which comes through Jesus Christ,
to the glory and praise of God."
—Philippians 1:9-11

And Job's plea was:

"Oh that my words were written!
Oh that they were inscribed in a book!
That with an iron stylus and lead
They were engraved in the rock forever!
As for me, I know that my Redeemer lives,
And at the last He will take His stand on the earth."
—Job 19:23-25

God granted Job's wish and preserved his life's story, as though engraved in rock for our learning and comfort. God provided this timeless epistle for us to be able to read and to understand more fully that with perseverance, we can say with conviction, "We have learned that serving God faithfully through any earthly valley can be endured, and spiritual growth can be our reward."

God Moves In A Mysterious Way

God moves in a mysterious way
His wonders to perform;
He plants His footsteps in the sea
And rides upon the storm.

Deep in unfathomable mines
Of never-failing skill
He treasures up His bright designs
And works His sovereign will.

Ye fearful saints, fresh courage take;
The clouds ye so much dread
Are big with mercy and shall break
In blessings on your head.

Judge not the Lord by feeble sense,
But trust Him for His grace;
Behind a frowning providence
He hides a smiling face.

His purposes will ripen fast,
Unfolding every hour;
The bud may have a bitter taste,
But sweet will be the flower.

Blind unbelief is sure to err
And scan His work in vain;
God is His own Interpreter,
And He will make it plain.
—William Cowper

ॐ

A Mother's Example of Faithful, Loving, Trusting Service

She was born July 1,1885, in Monticello, Iowa. Her parents chose to name her Margaret (beautiful gem) Lynne (abundant blessing). Her twin brother, Lloyd, was a sickly child, requiring most of her mother's time and attention.

With her parents and seven older brothers and sisters, she was brought by a covered wagon to Kansas when she was less than a year old. Because of her brother's illness, her oldest sister was assigned the duty of caring for her. This lowly, and perhaps lonely, beginning in life may have helped prepare her to accept the very difficult valleys that lay ahead.

After graduating, from high school and regular school, she taught school for a few years. (Her salary was $52.00 a month.) She met and married Tom, May 6, 1908. Their first child (Wendell) was born the following year.

Their second child, Opal Louise, was born on December 15, 1910. She was a beautiful baby with blonde hair that curled and deep blue eyes. She was delicately angelic in appearance.

Her younger brother, Raymond, arrived on November 5, 1912.

Tom had recently been diagnosed as having a very serious sinus infection and underlying bone disease and suffered from the resulting painful arthritis in his back.

He had been half-owner of what had been a very successful grocery store; but a severe 1911-1912 rabbit infestation in western Kansas had ravaged all the grass and anything else that was small and green. This had severely affected their customer's income so for now, the staples would remain on their shelves. Tom felt he had no choice but to sell his half interest to his co-owner's father and look for employment elsewhere.

He applied for a job with the railroad in a city a few miles away and was quickly accepted, allowing him to move his family to within a short distance of Lynne's parents. To Lynne's dismay, the new residence was infested with bedbugs, another challenge for her to overcome!

He was a dependable, hard-working man and soon advanced to foreman of the freight depot. This upgrade would require him to do some heavy lifting and work long strenuous hours, but the raise in pay was compelling.

When Opal was almost 3 years old, she suddenly became violently ill. The doctor was quickly summoned but he could find no cause for the obviously very serious illness. Both Tom and Lynne were feeling anxious and desperate as other doctors joined in the search for a cause. Three days after the onset of the illness (October 16, 1913) Opal died of an unknown cause. Tom and Lynne were completely unprepared, stunned and emotionally devastated. Days and nights were filled with indescribable grief and sorrow that refused to diminish. Lynne was unable to attend the funeral, as Raymond was now also very sick. Missing the final service for her precious little girl would take another toll on her grieving process. Adding to Lynne's distress, Wendell managed to swallow a needle. His memory of that event was having to swallow something that reminded him of cotton and milk.

About a year later, (1914) Lynne's 29-year-old twin brother died of appendicitis following a year-long illness. And the next year: March 10,1915, her father died suddenly of a stroke.

By this time Lynne had known for three months she was expecting another child. Maxine was born Oct 17 just as Wendell was recovering from whooping cough. The baby's strength as well as Lynne's was soon to be tested. Maxine began to cough deeply. For the next week the baby's deep cough was frightening to Lynne, and sleep was elusive. Only gratitude to God could be on her lips when the baby survived.

The following year was a continual nightmare for her as she saw Tom's health and strength decline. The children contracted red measles, German measles and chicken pox. Their day and night care rested solely on her shoulders, leaving her exhausted, but again, prayers of gratitude would follow.

In the summer of 1917, a decision was made to move to a farm near the Oklahoma, Kansas border. Tom's health could no longer tolerate the strenuous supervisory job for the railroad. He had been able to save enough money to buy cattle, chickens and two riding horses.

This move created even more hardships for Lynne. The old farmhouse was in a late stage of disrepair with large knotholes in the bare wood floors. In the winter, water froze in the buckets inside the drafty house. The extreme cold caused Tom's body to ache like it had never ached before, and sleep for him was impossible for many hours at a time. Mattresses were straw-filled, adding to his discomfort. Lynne would be up frequently, warming her handmade blankets by the wood stove to warm him as much as she could.

In the spring, they found another farm in Oklahoma that Tom thought would have more productive ground, but the old decaying house had only two rooms and a loft that was to be the bedroom for the two boys. Lynne was now expecting another child and the old house, with sagging doors, was deeply disappointing and discouraging. In winter, snow drifted in through the leaky roof and settled on the boys as they attempted to keep warm enough to sleep. Food was scarce, requiring Tom and Wendell to hunt wild game to keep the family from starving. Lynne had to spend some of her nights sewing clothing while the children slept. The light from the old gasoline lantern was dim, making her job even more difficult, and the old sewing machine required her already tired legs and feet to ache as they worked the treadle that powered it.

Lyda Kathleen (Katie) was born June 29,1918, just one year after the move from Kansas. Even material for diapers was scarce, causing Lynne to have to wash more often. The water well was about a half-mile from the house in a rattlesnake-infested pasture, making it challenging to have enough water for their needs.

The winter of 1918-1919 proved to be another nightmare for them. First, there was the terrible blizzard that left snow so deep it covered the fences, and all the cattle wandered off to neighboring farms. This was followed by a flu epidemic that caused all the children to become ill at once. Lynne had to climb the difficult wooden stairs to the loft to care for the two boys. The beds were full of sick children, including the baby, leaving no time for Lynne herself to get enough rest.

In the spring of 1920, Lynne's brother, Jim, offered for them to move to his farm in south central Kansas. This was great news, even though it would be very difficult to move the children and all their possessions in box wagons, and to herd their cattle; but they could look forward to a warmer house and better farmland.

By now, Tom had endured two surgeries to remove diseased bone from his face. Doctors had given him no hope for a less painful future. They were simply attempting to prolong his life.

February 22, 1921, now back in Kansas, they welcomed baby David. There was now more work in Lynne's life than she could possibly handle. Tom was having to make frequent trips to a distant hospital for more surgeries to remove more of the diseased bone. At this point, his suffering was so intense Lynne felt she must go with him each time he was admitted to the hospital to be at his side until he could return home. There was no doubt their love for each other continued undiminished.

When David was 3 years old, Lynne was again pregnant, and the doctors gave her the unwelcome news she must have surgery immediately to remove a large goiter. She survived the surgery, but this illness added to their already huge hospital bill.

Eugene arrived January 30,1925. He was a fretful child, requiring day and night care. The removal of Lynne's goiter while pregnant was deemed to be responsible for Eugene's irritability. Just two months later, March 29, Lynne's brother sold the farm they were living on to his son. Lynne and Tom were now facing another dreaded move.

After the move was finally complete, January 19, 1926, Margaret was born. The now brilliantly white-haired Lynne was just 41 years old, and Eugene was just one year old. Eleven-year-old Maxine would happily assume much of the care for this new, and final, baby.

By now, Tom had received some discouraging news concerning his health: the disease in his face was no longer treatable and his time to live was limited. The throbbing pain was becoming unbearable, but he would live and suffer for almost six more long years. He died in 1931, just prior to Christmas. (Many years later, a doctor who had been our neighbor, informed me that my father had died of cancer. I had no way to prove this as all the hospital records had been destroyed in a flood.) Lynne, though mourning for her beloved Tom, would do what she could to provide a small Christmas for her now fatherless children; but the small gifts did little to take away the sadness that hung heavily over herself and the children. The neighbor, their barber, the caring friend everyone knew as "Little Tom," was gone! The loving father and encourager would no longer be available to Lynne and the children in times of trouble! A tragic, irreplaceable loss.

Lynne had been aware for a few months that she needed surgery to remove a large abdominal precancerous tumor. This surgery proved to be near fatal for her due to unexpected hemorrhaging. And more dollars were added to the looming hospital bill.

Lynne must now persevere alone, counting every penny the farm could produce in order to start paying the huge debts that remained. The hospital offered to forgive the debt, but Lynne refused the offer, saying it was an honest debt and she would pay it!

Lynne continued to live on the farm, doing a man's work much of the time: shocking oats, shoveling wheat, hoeing the garden, mending fences, canning meats, vegetables and fruits, and sewing: she would work with and for her children to complete each waiting task.

When Margaret was sixteen, Lynne decided to send her to live with her sister. At this age she could support herself.

Lynne and Gene would continue to live on the farm for two more years, until she made the decision to sell all the farm equipment, the livestock and everything she owned, except her clothing. With this money, she paid the remaining debt at the hospital and moved to a room in the town that she and Tom had lived in before moving to the first farm. Here, she would wash dishes at a restaurant, living a lonely life of hard work for little pay.

Her later years were spent living with Margaret and her husband, John, until she needed more care than they could provide. Her last residence was a nursing home back in the town she was living in when her baby Opal had died.

Her trust in God had remained undiminished through every stage of her very difficult lifetime. Prayers of gratitude before meals were not to be overlooked even though the food on the farm was often just enough to keep hunger from taking away energy to work. Whether or not the family was going to worship God on Sunday morning was never a question. They would go if at all possible.

I hope her story of *It Can Be Done* is an encouragement to all who read it. It was God's blessing to me to be Tommy and Lynne's youngest child.

It Is Well With My Soul

When peace like a river attendeth my way,
When sorrows like sea billows roll;
Whatever my lot, Thou hast taught me to say,
"It is well, it is well, with my soul."

My sin–O the bliss of this glorious tho't–
My sin, not in part but the whole,
Is nailed to the cross and I bear it no more;
Praise the Lord, praise the Lord, O my soul!

And, Lord, haste the day when the faith shall be sight,
The clouds be rolled back like a scroll,
The trump shall resound and the Lord shall descend,
"Even so"–it is well with my soul.
–H.G. Spafford

Chapter 4

Lovingly Assisting Others Who Are in Valleys of Distress

*"Bear (Carry, NIV) one another's burdens,
and thereby fulfill the law of Christ."*
—Galatians 6:2

જી

*"Let us not lose heart in doing good, for in
due time we will reap if we do not grow weary.
So then, while we have opportunity, let us do good
to all people, and especially to those who are of the
household of the faith."*
—Galatians 6:9-10

જી

To fairly assess the needs of another, our first obligation to them is to listen intently, with love, kindness and empathy in our own non-judgmental hearts.

*"He who gives an answer before he hears,
It is folly and shame to him."*
—Proverbs 18:13

This scripture is indeed a gold nugget that could save many misunderstandings and hurt feelings!

Quiet answers, patience, and prayer may be the key to calming stress and anxiety experienced by the person(s) we want to help. There may be times when this is all that is required for them to see their way to exit their valleys successfully without dependence on others.

"The lips of the righteous feed many,
But fools die for lack of understanding."
—Proverbs 10:21

This passage warns us we could become one of the "fools" if we lack understanding. Too, it is very unwise, hurtful, and foolish to share what should be kept private!

We have no real control over the poor choices others may finally make, which could cause us to become discouraged if we allow it, but we can find comfort by praying they will see the error of making inappropriate decisions. If we are honest with ourselves, we are probably going to have to admit we have made some unwise choices during our lifetime, also. But our blessing is; *"If I should say, 'My foot has slipped,' Your lovingkindness, O Lord, will hold me up" (Psalm 94:18)..*

> "Maturity comes from actions carefully
> considered beforehand and then carefully
> evaluated afterward."
> —GaryHenry

To help us feel more confident about the choices we make concerning those we may need to assist, the account of the good Samaritan supplies us with valuable nuggets to add to our collection from other scriptures: Luke 10:25-37 - *"And a lawyer (an expert in the law, NIV) stood up and put Him to the test, saying, "Teacher, what shall I do to inherit eternal life?" And He said to him, "What is written in the law? How does it read to you?" And he answered, "YOU SHALL LOVE THE LORD YOUR GOD WITH ALL YOUR HEART, AND WITH ALL YOUR SOUL, AND WITH ALL YOUR STRENGTH, AND WITH ALL YOUR MIND; AND YOUR NEIGHBOR AS YOURSELF." And He said to him, "You have answered correctly; DO THIS AND YOU WILL LIVE." But wishing to justify himself, he said to Jesus, "And who is my neighbor?"* (Now the lawyer is the one who is about to be tested.) *Jesus replied and said, "A man was going down from Jerusalem to Jericho, and fell among robbers, and they stripped him and beat him, and went away leaving him half dead. And by chance a priest was going down on that road, and when he saw him, he passed by on the other side. Likewise, a Levite also, when he came to the place and saw him, passed by on the other side."* (These two men, who should have been devoutly religious servants of God, showed no compassion or mercy.)

Let's look down into that ditch from the other side of the road and ask ourselves if we would have reacted as the next passerby did, OR would we have been among those who simply walked on without pity on the other side of the road. (Remember, we are looking at a stranger that has been stripped of his clothing, bleeding, lying in a ditch, half dead. A very depressing, discouraging, and unappealing sight!) This is a REAL test of servitude Jesus is proposing!

"But a Samaritan, (who would have been looked down on by the priest and the Levite) who was on a journey, came upon him; and when he saw him, he felt compassion, and came to him and bandaged up his wounds, pouring oil and wine on them; (This would have required time and patience, considering the condition of the patient.) *and he put him on his own beast,* (this, too, was a sacrifice on his part as he was probably wearing sandals on this rocky, descending road) *and brought him to an inn and took care of him. On the next day he took out two denarii and gave them to the innkeeper and said, 'Take care of him; and whatever more you spend, when I return I will repay you.' Which of these three do you think proved to be a neighbor to the man who fell into the robbers' hands?" And he said, 'The one who showed mercy toward him.' Then Jesus said to him, 'Go and do the same.'"* This last statement made by Jesus was a command. This man's salvation depended on his "doing the same." But I should remember, this was recorded for "my" learning, also.

The gold nuggets we find in this account are many. This road where the injured man was found ran through a rocky desert land where robbers took advantage of defenseless travelers. This Samaritan had to be willing to take the risk of being robbed himself to take care of a half dead man. (Am I willing to take risks to help strangers?) He could have reasoned; the man may have been carrying drugs, so why try to help someone like this? Or he might have reasoned that he did not have time to take care of him. Instead, he spent the night at the inn caring for this total stranger.

Do I use the "too busy" excuse? "Too tired?" Or am I just "uncaring"? The good Samaritan gave the innkeeper two silver coins which probably amounted to two days' wages. This was no small donation; and he was coming back to pay more if needed. How often do I zip my purse closed instead of helping those in need? Do I have just a little bit of that "service destroying love of money" in my heart? From Jesus' final reply,

I should be willing to go and do as the good Samaritan did. His service came from a very humble and unselfish heart. I need to ask myself if my hardened heart is begging for the blood of Christ to cleanse it from the sin of selfishness.

> *"For just as the body without the spirit is dead,*
> *so also faith without works is dead."*
> —James 2:26

Note that nationality was not a consideration in the narrative of the good Samaritan.

> *"Here there is no Greek or Jew, circumcised*
> *or uncircumcised, barbarian, Scythian, slave*
> *or free, but Christ is all, and is in all."*
> —Colossians 3:11 (NIV)

"So speak and so act as those who are to be judged by the law of liberty. For judgment will be merciless to one who has shown no mercy; mercy triumphs over judgment" (James 2:12-13). "Never pay back evil for evil to anyone. Respect what is right in the sight of all men. If possible, so far as it depends on you, be at peace with all men. Never take your own revenge, beloved, but leave room for the wrath of God, for it is written, "VENGEANCE IS MINE, I WILL REPAY," says the Lord. BUT IF YOUR ENEMY IS HUNGRY, FEED HIM, AND IF HE IS THIRSTY, GIVE HIM A DRINK; FOR IN SO DOING YOU WILL HEAP BURNING COALS ON HIS HEAD" (Romans 12:17-20).

Scripture does not reveal this, but the Good Samaritan may have assisted an enemy, just as God would have us do.

The nuggets we have gleaned from mining the account of the Good Samaritan should be all the guidance we need in helping others in their similar or even less drastic circumstances. If we follow the Good Samaritans' example, we may find ourselves being more watchful for ways to serve others.

One way to lovingly and carefully consider is looking after widows and orphans as it is a task that can be easily overlooked or taken lightly. It is easy to fail to give enough of our time to resolve their needs completely.

*"Religion that God our Father accepts
as pure and faultless is this: to look
after orphans and widows in their
distress and to keep oneself from
being polluted by the world."*
—James 1:27(NIV)

Their valleys are some of the most difficult to escape. (I have experienced and endured this indescribable valley, but how much easier God's loving care and that of His servants made it to endure!)

The Old Testament brings to our awareness God's love and concern for the needy widows and orphans. Let us bow to his authority as he leads us in paths of righteousness. *"Then I will draw near to you for judgment; and I will be a swift witness against the sorcerers and against the adulterers and against those who swear falsely, and against those who oppress the wage earner in his wages, the widow and the orphan, and those who turn aside the alien and do not fear Me," says the Lord of hosts"* (Malachi 3:5).

*"Cursed is he who distorts the justice
due an alien, orphan, and widow.
And all the people shall say, 'Amen."*
—Deuteronomy 27:19)

Both widows and orphans miss the companionship, warmth, and the love they were hopefully accustomed to receiving. Even if they were not loved, they are in critical need of it at this point in their lives. This "looking after" is a direct command God expects us to honor. (But, let us remember there is a difference between meddling and assisting.) Young children will probably have some very special needs being overlooked by the parent because of their own grief. Remember, many times, children's valleys are more difficult because of their lack of understanding of the love of God. This is a very special opportunity to lighten their concerns by telling them of the love and merciful compassion of God and outwardly assuring them of our love and concern for them. Love speaks in many ways: our time, comforting words, our touch, small gifts, even as little as a bowl of warm soup are our expression of the love they need so much to feel. How can we speak to them of God's love if we do not live by His example?

We can also mine the narrative of Lazarus' death for nuggets concerning Jesus' mercy and gain from His example of tender love and compassion (John 11:1- 45).

For Him to offer comfort to Mary and Martha, Jesus would have to travel back to Judea where unbelievers had tried to stone him. This threat did not deter his plan to go to those he loved. (Do I allow smaller obstacles than this to get in the way of my comforting deeds?) *"Martha then said to Jesus, 'Lord, if You had been here, my brother would not have died'" (John 11:21).*

We learn in prior verses that his death was according to God's plan. Do we ever assume we know things God has done? If so, Satan is again involved in one of his soul-destroying schemes to trap us.

"When Jesus therefore saw her (Mary) *weeping, and the Jews who came with her also weeping, He was deeply moved in spirit and was troubled, and said, 'Where have you laid him?' They said to Him, 'Lord, come and see.' Jesus wept" (vv. 33-35).* Jesus' example of weeping with and for his friends gives us insight that this is "how" He would have us help relieve the stress of troubled hearts. *"Rejoice with those who rejoice, and weep with those who weep" (Romans 12:15).* May we never be ashamed of the loving, caring tears we shed as we mourn with and for others.

"So the Jews were saying, 'See how He loved him!' But some of them said, 'Could not this man, who opened the eyes of the blind man, have kept this man also from dying?'" (John 11:36-37). This account, itself, has answered that question for us. But who are we that we should ever question our God? If we are mourning for someone who died, we do not need to question God. As we learned from Job, God does not need to be questioned. His ways are perfect.

> *"As for God, His way is blameless;*
> *The word of the Lord is tested; (flawless, NIV);*
> *He is a shield to all who take refuge in Him."*
> *—2 Samuel 22:31*

Following are some of my thoughts concerning those needing help from others after a death: remember, they are dealing with a broken heart. Understanding sympathy is their basic need.

- First, we must respect their boundaries and make sure we are not interfering. If they do need and accept our help, we may have to determine their needs concerning some, or all, of the following:
- Money/financial needs or guidance—they may need help to find other readily available resources for money or guidance.
- Other business affairs: they may need and accept help to update their will, help to make sure bills are paid, change name on bank account(s), annuities, car title, loans, property deed. etc. We could cause a problem by suggesting who to place on legal documents. This needs to be carefully considered and decided by the owner. (A copy of the death certificate will be necessary to make these changes.) They may also need help notifying Social Security for burial funds, etc. They will probably need to draft a new will.
- Do they need help collecting insurance and making updates/both life and medical insurance?
- Do they need meals or have food allergies?
- Supply special foods, if required.
- Shopping for personal needs may be necessary.
- Offer transportation to medical appointments, worship services, etc.
- Offer Bible study in their home.
- Do they need help with problem-solving, child care, or help with thank-you notes? Let's be very specific about what we want to offer so the recipient can be sure this fills a need. But again, please attend to the needs of the children!
- Do they need prescriptions for medications, refills, or help to dispose of medications of the deceased? (Do not flush or put medication in the trash. Many drug stores can solve this problem by asking them how.)
- Perhaps helping them make and execute a move to a care facility is needed. (We can locate and visit facilities with them.) If they request or accept this offer, we can pray with them before beginning the search for the home, and continue to visit them after the move.
- Our obligation is to stay involved until meeting their needs. This may be the most important reminder I

have mentioned. The deep grieving will probably last for months, so learning to live with it is the key to going forward with their lives. During this time of learning, they will have a deep need to know others are aware of their sorrow, who care enough to keep in touch. This is a time to keep them involved in good deeds when they are able. Keeping them involved will cause them to feel needed and useful, and spiritual growth and diminishing grief will usually be the welcome end-result.

All that should be expected in return for any help rendered to others is simple gratitude. If this is not forthcoming, we can thank God we had the privilege of being His servant.

In time we may personally need to become grateful, easy to care for, accepting recipients of the care provided for us. As an example of this kind of care:

"I was very ill in a hospital; too sick to feed myself. A precious friend, without being asked, prepared food and drove the long distance to the hospital and stayed to feed me." This was an act of kindness that I am unable to repay; nor can it be erased from my grateful heart and mind.

> *"But as for you, brethren,*
> *do not grow weary of doing good."*
> *—2 Thessalonians 3:13*

If we follow the above examples of love and availability, we will always be ready to assist others, if possible. May we be careful to search out these needs and respond appropriately. Remember, the need for intimacy starts with birth and only ends at death; prayers, hugs, and loving words are a real need we should remember to fill.

Some may be hesitant to ask us for our help: we will need to call them or go to their home to offer help.

We may also need to be careful that we are not just being used as enablers instead of being the needed helpers and teachers God would have us to be. However, when in doubt, we may serve their needs as the Good Samaritan did, without complaining or being judgmental. Do

I ever share my good deeds with others to hear their praise? The devil is there, waiting.

> *"In everything, therefore, treat people*
> *the same way you want them to treat you,*
> *for this is the Law and the Prophets."*
> —Matthew 7:12

Following is another glimpse into the emotionally and physically painful valley David and Rhonda continued to endure bravely. They do not seek or desire praise as they shared only at my request!

Journal entry by David Ditter, dated 12/8/2016

"To this point, we have no further information concerning the forecast of clinical trial participation. Of course, waiting to hear is difficult, wishing to prepare for whatever is on the horizon. Rhonda has had her ups and downs in how she has been feeling and what she has been able to accomplish since the last update. She has had the pleasure of visits from a few saints, being lavished with gifts of love and the yearning of their hearts. Her appetite remains strong and her resolve is as well. Rhonda is ready to take on whatever lies before her, as a result of the peace of God and the supply of His strength, that which all of you have been pleading with God, on Rhonda's behalf, Wonderful, Merciful Savior. I encourage all of you to continue your fervent and tireless effort, not only for Rhonda, but for yourselves as well. Let us all not grow weary, trusting in the Lord with all of our heart, knowing that he cares for us. We Love you all."

ಬ

In Heavenly Love Abiding

In heavenly love abiding,
No change my heart shall fear;
And safe is such confiding,
For nothing changes here.

The storm may roar without me,
My heart may low be laid,
But God is round about me,
And can I be dismayed?

Wherever He may guide me,
No want shall turn me back;
My Shepherd is beside me,
And nothing can I lack.

His wisdom ever waketh,
His sight is never dim;
He knows the way He taketh,
And I will walk with Him.

Green pastures are before me,
Which yet I have not seen.
Bright skies will soon be o'er me,
Where the dark clouds have been.

My hope I cannot measure,
My path to life is free;
My Savior has my treasure,
And He will walk with me.
–Anna L. Waring

Chapter 5

The Heartbreaking Valleys of Broken Relationships

If someone approaches us concerning a broken relationship, it will be wise for us to be very careful that we are not also caught up in the sin that caused the problem. Even a misunderstanding can become sinful in the way it is approached or handled. Have we become judgmental, angry, or gossipers? Without their permission to share their problem with others, it is hurtful and unkind to do so. *"He who conceals a transgression seeks love, but he who repeats a matter separates intimate friends" (Proverbs 17:9).* The same Satan who tempted Job has been at work to place new victims in his sinful traps, and he will continue to tempt and frustrate those in distress, sadly. He will attempt to do the same for those who lovingly attempt to help them to higher ground.

> *"Blessed are the peacemakers,*
> *for they shall be called sons of God."*
> *—Matthew 5:9*

Of course, we fail as peacemakers if we, too, fall into sin with faulty counseling.

Broken relationships can become some of the most emotionally challenging valleys to escape. Pride truly deserves its place at the top of most lists of problems involved.

> *"Pride goes before destruction,*
> *And a haughty spirit before stumbling."*
> *—Proverbs 16:18*

ॐ

> *"When pride comes, then comes dishonor (disgrace, NIV),*
> *But with the humble is wisdom."*
> *—Proverbs 11:2*

How many times have we stumbled because we did not humbly seek and apply God's wisdom? A troubling thought!

The book of Proverbs is also rich in information and instruction concerning the tongue that can be used for healing others.

"A gentle answer turns away wrath,
but a harsh word stirs up anger.
The tongue of the wise makes knowledge acceptable,
but the mouth of fools spouts folly."
—Proverbs 15:1-2

ജ

"A perverse man spreads strife, and a
slanderer separates intimate friends."
—Proverbs 16:28

God's wisdom regarding the tongue's ability to heal is deeply rewarding to us if heeded. He also warns it is so very easy for us to misuse our tongue and become a part of the sin involved! James' warning and admonition: *"And the tongue is a fire, the very world of iniquity (evil, NIV); the tongue is set among our members (the parts of the body, NIV) as that which defiles the entire body, and sets on fire the course of our life, and is set on fire by hell"* (James 3:6). This is a GRIM admonition showing how easy it is for us to allow Satan to win the battle in our heated or even petty disputes. And Peter's instruction: *"For, "THE ONE WHO DESIRES LIFE, TO LOVE AND SEE GOOD DAYS, MUST KEEP HIS TONGUE FROM EVIL AND HIS LIPS FROM SPEAKING DECEIT"* (1 Peter 3:10).

The following scripture reveals how great the wisdom of God is in preventing or healing broken relationships. And heal them they must, if at all possible. Precious souls are at stake.

"Love is patient, love is kind and is not jealous;
love does not brag and is not arrogant, does not
act unbecomingly; it does not seek its own, is not
provoked, does not take into account a wrong suffered,
does not rejoice in unrighteousness, but rejoices with

the truth; bears all things, believes all things, hopes
all things, endures all things."
—*1 Corinthians 13:4-7*

Are we not able to feel the healing power of God's wisdom in His inter-pretation of true, acceptable love?

The outline provided below is a scriptural pattern the Holy Spirit has outlined for Christians to use to resolve disagreements or broken rela-tionships (Matthew, chapters 15 through 18).

1. Looking for the root of the problem I am experiencing should cause me to examine my heart and to ask myself; "has my brother (or sister) sinned against me?" If not, I need to im-mediately forgive him/her and look into my own heart to see why I have allowed myself to become so easily offended. I must repent and pray.

2. However, if I am convinced he has sinned against me, am I able to use scripture to demonstrate he has sinned? If not, I am exhibiting a spiritual weakness that I need to address and eliminate thoroughly. This, too, calls for repentance and prayer: Love does not take into account a wrong suffered.

3. If yes, he has sinned against me: *"If your brother sins, go and show him his fault in private" (Mt 18:15a).* This will protect both of us from becoming the target of ungodly, soul taint-ing gossip. If he listens, I have won my brother over, and now is the time for rejoicing! (Showing another their fault takes courage, but I must persevere in my service to God. Other-wise, I may also be living in sin: love is kind.

4. Am I lacking the qualities of love I should have for him since he has repented? Do I have a beam in my eye? If yes, I need to continue to work on my own self-righteous, sinful attitude. *"Why do you look at the speck that is in your brother's eye, but do not notice the log that is in your own eye" (Matthew 7:3)?*

5. Do I have reason to fear for my safety or that of my children? Has he physically abused any of us in the past? If not, then

what is my reason for fearing him? Is it unfounded, or is it a warning to seek help?

6. If he has a problem with anger and has harmed the children or me, I must kindly approach him about his sinful act. If he repents and asks forgiveness, I must faithfully forgive him. However, if the abuse continues, you would be wise to seek help unless he agrees to counseling. Love does not act unbecomingly.

"But if he does not listen to you, take one or two more with you, so that BY THE MOUTH OF TWO OR THREE WITNESSES EVERY FACT MAY BE CONFIRMED" (Matthew 18:16). Did this cause him to repent of any sin against me? If so, I can now rejoice that he has been restored! And if he repents, even the angels in heaven will rejoice with us. *"Or what woman, if she has ten silver coins and loses one coin, does not light a lamp and sweep the house and search carefully until she finds it? When she has found it, she calls together her friends and neighbors, saying, 'Rejoice with me, for I have found the coin which I had lost!' In the same way, I tell you, there is joy in the presence of the angels of God over one sinner who repents"* (Luke 15:8-10). *"If he refuses to listen even to the church, let him be to you as a Gentile and a tax collector"* (Matthew 18:17b). Now our hearts will weep for the lost soul and we must pray for his hardened heart to become penitent; but until that takes place, sadly, we must withdraw from him. He has rejected counsel given by our all-wise God. *"Then Peter came and said to Him, 'Lord, how often shall my brother sin against me and I forgive him? Up to seven times?' Jesus said to him, 'I do not say to you, up to seven times, but up to seventy times seven'"* (Matthew 18:21-22).

I must be willing to accept the above command concerning forgiveness, or I will be living in sin.

"Hatred stirs up strife,
but love covers all transgressions."
—Proverbs 10:12

Other sins that can damage or destroy relationships include looking at pornography (immorality), swearing, and vulgar jokes (impurity). And what about filthiness, silly talk, and coarse jesting? These will cause us to become sons of disobedience.

*"But immorality or any impurity or greed
must not even be named among you, as is proper
among saints; and there must be no filthiness and
silly talk, or coarse jesting, which are not fitting,
but rather giving of thanks. For this you know with
certainty, that no immoral or impure person or covetous
man, who is an idolater, has an inheritance
in the kingdom of Christ and God.
Let no one deceive you with empty words,
for because of these things the wrath of God
comes upon the sons of disobedience.
Therefore do not be partakers with them."*
—Ephesians 5:3-7

And what about the books we are reading? Are they filling our minds with good or with the devil's trash?

Satan maximizes the use of these deceitful tools to lure God's servants to forsake their good reputations and fall into his dangerous, soul-destroying traps.

*"Be merciful to those who doubt; snatch others from
the fire and save them; to others show mercy, mixed
with fear – hating even the clothing
stained by corrupted flesh."*
—Jude 22-23 NIV

*"Watch over your heart with all diligence, for from it flow
the springs of life. Put away from you a deceitful mouth
(corrupt talk, NIV) And put devious speech far from you."*
—Proverbs 4:23-24

Until now, I have avoided addressing what is probably the most "family-destroying" of all valleys to fall into—the valley of divorce! And it is one of the most repugnant to me since it has left its debasing mark on my own family. It is one of the most diabolical tools for the destruction of family ties the devil has cleverly chosen to implement!

If we are living our marriage in accordance with God's word, we may be asked to counsel someone concerning their marriage problems. If we are not extremely wise about what we advise, we may find ourselves adding to their existing problem and ourselves having to repent of our fallible counseling. Prejudice (pre-judging) is a sin that builds a solid wall of resistance and prevents any problem-solving. I must not allow even a trace of this in my own heart.

The following passage is filled with all the pure gold nuggets we will need to embrace to keep our marriages intact. This, of course, requires both parties to be willing to embrace it: *"Now the deeds of the flesh are evident, which are: immorality, impurity, sensuality, idolatry, sorcery, enmities, strife, jealousy, outbursts of anger, disputes, dissensions, factions, envying, drunkenness, carousing, and things like these, of which I forewarn you, just as I have forewarned you, that those who practice such things will not inherit the kingdom of God. But the fruit of the Spirit is love, joy, peace, patience, kindness, goodness, faithfulness, gentleness, self-control; against such things there is no law"* (Galatians 5:19-23).

How very easy it is to get caught up in a heated dispute or faction! Only God's truths, if heeded, promote healing, comforting peace.

The following passages reveal why God hates divorce: *"It was said, 'WHOEVER SENDS HIS WIFE AWAY, LET HIM GIVE HER A CERTIFICATE OF DIVORCE'; but I say to you that everyone who divorces his wife, except for the reason of unchastity, makes her commit adultery; and whoever marries a divorced woman commits adultery"* (Matthew 5:31-32). *"Now God has not only raised the Lord, but will also raise us up through His power. Do you not know that your bodies are members of Christ? Shall I then take away the members of Christ and make them members of a prostitute? May it never be! Or do you not know that the one who joins himself to a prostitute is one body with her? For He says, "THE TWO SHALL BECOME ONE FLESH." But the one who joins himself to the Lord is one spirit with Him"* (1 Corinthians 6:14-17). This scripture is a stern warning! May we incline our hearts to yearn for and accept God's wisdom.

Consider the toll the parents' divorce can place on their children:

Divorce deprives children of the comfort of a healthy home atmosphere, and for many, it will undermine their sense of emotional stability. Most feel unloved, others may also feel neglected and betrayed, and some feel guilty that they may have been the cause of all or part of the problem(s).

The majority lose their ability to concentrate at school, so they usually have lower academic scores.

Some are very badly mistreated. Most are juggled from one parent to the other or to grandparents, leaving them without the choice of where they live or of making plans of their own.

Some are forced to endure the anger and jealousy of a step-parent or their step-parent's children, while others will have to live in the home of a relative that may not love or even want them.

When a father or mother leaves the union, the mother or father who stays with the children may take on being a friend to the child/children and desert the father/mother role. This is a very damaging role the parent has accepted, as this will usually result in a lack of much-needed discipline for the child/children.

Very few divorces take place because of children. The children are simply the recipients of divorce fallout.

How cruel, uncaring, and selfish have we become that we could treat innocent children in this inhumane, ungodly manner?

"At that time the disciples came to Jesus and said,
'Who then is greatest in the kingdom of heaven?'
And He called a child to Himself and set him before them,
and said, 'Truly I say to you, unless you are converted
and become like children,
you will not enter the kingdom of heaven.
Whoever then humbles himself as this child,
he is the greatest in the kingdom of heaven.
And whoever receives one such child
in My name receives Me;

but whoever causes one of these little ones
who believes in Me to stumble,
it would be better for him to have a heavy millstone
hung around his neck,
and to be drowned in the sea.'"
—*Matthew 18:1-6*

જી

A Little Child

Give me a little child to point the way
Over strange, sweet paths that lead to Thee;
Give me a little voice to teach to pray:
Give me two shining eyes Thy face to see.

The only crown I ask, dear Lord, to wear
Is this: that I may teach a little child
How beautiful, how divinely fair
Is Thy dear face, so loving, sweet and mild.

I do not need to ask for more than this:
My opportunity? It's standing at my door.
What sorrow if this blessing I should miss!
A little child! Why should I ask for more?
—Author unknown

જી

"Behold, children are a gift of the Lord,
The fruit of the womb is a reward."
—*Psalm 127:3*

જી

"But if you have bitter jealousy and selfish ambition in your heart,
do not be arrogant and so lie against the truth.
This wisdom is not that which comes down from above,
but is earthly, natural, demonic.
For where jealousy and selfish ambition exist,
there is disorder and every evil thing."
—*James 3:14-16*

I must be very careful to guard my heart against jealousy! It is a relationship-destroying tool Satan has great success promoting.

Divorce for any reason causes devastation in the lives of ALL concerned; whether parents, children, grandparents, friends, or all relatives: all are adversely emotionally, and for some, spiritually affected. Holidays, marriages, vacations, birthdays, and other usually happy occasions are marred or may even become family battlegrounds when divorce rears its ugly head. Please! All married couples, watch for and heed all of God's STOP signs. Like Job, who made a covenant with his eyes, take this a step further and make a covenant with your bodies!

The following is, sadly, a true narrative shared by Michael Moore:

> "One of the worst moments of my life was when my wife told me she did not love me, but thought she loved one of her students. (She was a professor at a community college.) We had only been married sixteen months.
>
> I was a relatively new Christian of three years and seven days. She grew up knowing the truth of the Gospel of Christ and was baptized as a teenager.
>
> On September 23rd we were on our way to Fort Smith, Arkansas, for the wedding of one of her best friends from college. We stopped in a nowhere place in Tennessee to stay at a Red Roof Inn. As we entered the rented room for the night, she looked around with disappointment and said what was in her heart, "I don't love you anymore. I think I love _____". Stunned, I just stopped and stood there for a few seconds wondering how to respond or handle her remark. Should I lash out with anger? Should I just pack the car back up and head back home to Florida? No was the answer to both questions. I went into the bathroom and closed the door and prayed. I had no words to offer back.

After getting some much-needed sleep, I decided to continue on to Fort Smith and checked into a hotel. Which hotel, I could not say. I was an empty shell at this point, just continuing with the purpose of why we were there.

We met with her college friends and spent the next day and a half visiting with them. During our stay she said she was confused and did love me, but those hollow words did not have the same impact as the words she had said the day before.

I simply endured the wedding on Saturday.

After assembling with saints on Sunday morning we started home. I had no desire to stop in Tennessee, so I drove straight through to Florida.

Days later she asked me if she could use her maiden name at the community college where she taught. She was not happy with my negative answer.

She asked if she could go over to her student's house to talk with him. I could not give her permission to do something I knew was wrong.

As time continued, I asked her if she was going to divorce me. Her response was heartless. Finally, on October 19, she left me. She had reached out to her college friends who were Christians and they also told her she was wrong to divorce me. They let the word of God guide them in what they advised her as I had done, but she refused to listen to them, as she had to me.

One day in November I was getting the mail out of the mailbox, feeling very down and alone, hoping to have a card of encouragement in the mail from one or more of my Christian brethren. But there were no cards. It came to me to stop looking for cards of encouragement and write my own cards to encourage a brother and a sister in Christ. So, that is what I did. The next Lord's day, when I entered the assembly, the brother and sister I had written to came to me and hugged me. They were astonished that I would write them when they felt they should have been writing to encourage me.

I continue to live alone, filling my life with service to God.

His word is true: "It is much better to give than to receive."
—Michael Moore

What did Michael learn from his valley of divorce?

- Each year when I receive my auto insurance renewal, I read how the insurance company sees me: male, xx years old, multiple policies, good driving record, no accidents; and 'divorced.'

- It pains me each time I receive it, because I am reminded that I failed as a husband.

- No, I was not unfaithful to her, but I was not the man I should have been as a husband. (Emotionally, an exceedingly tough lesson to learn!)

- I was young in the faith and had some of the 'old self' in me and was still learning to 'put on the new' (Ephesians 4:22-24).

- However, that lack of maturity in my spirituality did not provide her with the right to divorce me.

- But God has called me to peace (1 Corinthians 7:15). (This was a comforting lesson learned.)

- He can still use me for His purpose and good as I remember how I am free to please the Lord. (And that is my goal.)

- Becoming more and more useful in God's kingdom helped heal the wounds left by the divorce (1 Corinthians 7:32).

- This has helped me change my valley into a value of learning and maturing, (and responding) spiritually.

- I am rejoicing that my name is recorded in Heaven, God's eternal blessing!
  —Michael Moore

Different in nature but comparative in terms of loss, the death of a lifelong partner also comes with a grieving process that can only be better endured by obediently trusting and serving God:

> In January 2007, my life dropped into a deep valley. My husband, Bruce, had shoulder surgery and was doing well in therapy. Suddenly, his body began to fill with fluid. On Friday, he was taken to his orthopedic doctor. He told us that the fluid buildup had nothing to do with the shoulder surgery and sent us to an oncologist. The oncologist looked at Bruce and quickly sent him to the hospital. He immediately called the hospital with orders for tests to begin as soon as we arrived. By Wednesday, Bruce was diagnosed with last-stage liver cancer. He was given six months to live, then three months, and finally weeks. I wanted him at home so I could take care of him. On Friday, he was sedated and sent home by ambulance. Hospice was waiting for us. At 1:30 Saturday morning, he passed away. He never woke up. My partner for nearly fifty years was gone!

I started my grieving period by thanking God for all the blessings he provided through my husband. He allowed me to have a godly man as a mate all those years, gave my children a loving, godly example, and gave us a man who worked so hard to provide for his family. I consider the time we had together a gift from God. I have tried to concentrate on my blessings instead of on the loneliness and self-pity. Therefore, it has been easier to accept the tragedy and to fill my life with adjustments, acceptance, and contentment.

Besides struggling for emotional strength to face life alone, I faced many difficult every-day problems to get my life in some sort of order. A good understanding lawyer helped me through most of the legal work in a timely manner. The key here was to not let my inexperience and frustration overtake me.

It would have been so much harder to accept my loss and make needed adjustments without God's help. He has promised to comfort us in all tribulation (II Cor. 1: 3-4). I strive to put my complete faith, hope, and trust in God, which prevents my heart from being overcome with frustration, confusion, and depression. He will never leave me and He knows and cares when I hurt. He always listens when the hour of my grief is so dark.

I realized that my life being turned upside down did not mean I ceased being a servant of the Lord: God should still be first in my life. I found that if I used my time of loneliness to be His servant by helping others in need, there was not much room left for self-pity and bitterness in my life. This led to the belief that there was actually a gift from God hidden in my tragedy. I am now called upon to help and comfort, with understanding, those who lose a spouse, especially the new widows who are struggling with so much emotional pain.

I was asked to participate in a lecture series in 2013 with the theme BUILD STRONG HOMES. My subject was "Adjusting to Widowhood." I have given this lecture to several groups of women around this county and one in Auburn, Alabama. These discussions are good reinforcements for me to be content with my state in life.

I cannot tell you that the days since I dropped into that "deep valley" were easy; but I can truthfully say that those years have been easier by concentrating on positive thoughts, helping others, and counting my blessings
—Ruby Hall

Ruby continues to have people she has counseled thank her for the emotional help and comfort she was able to provide them for a persevering recovery.

My plea to anyone considering divorce is that you will reconsider and make it your priority to make your marriage work. If you are just unhappy, then remind yourself that happiness is a choice and is the proper choice God would have us make.

One can only find true happiness in Him.

Sadly, we must accept the reality that there are times when divorce is inevitable and must be accepted. God's word and prayer should make this decision to divorce clear to us.

If mental illness is the cause of the problem, you may need to seek help. There are prescription drugs available that may be helpful to allow that person to fulfill their part of the marriage in a very satisfactory manner. If that is not successful, the well partner will probably need to seek the help of the elders of the church for emotional and spiritual help and seek professional help as well. Emotional instability only does not give the partner the right to seek a divorce. You may not be able to share the same household if the ill partner is a threat to the children.

To those in a valley due to a broken relationship, I ask that you continue to diligently study God's word for answers and make every effort to apply His wisdom to your heart and thus to the problem. Most importantly, persevere in serving God.

How good it is when we can exonerate (forgive, pardon) one another, never to bring an incident up again. If you have a problem with anger or forgiveness, you are invited to take your heart to the foot of the cross of Jesus; and as you kneel there in subjection to His will, you will be able to hear Him ask God to forgive those who were crucifying him. The anger will submit to peace, and forgiveness will follow. *"Be kind to one another, tender-hearted, forgiving each other, just as God in Christ also has forgiven you"* (Ephesians 4:32). *"But Jesus was saying, 'Father, forgive them, for they do not know what they are doing'"* (Luke 23:34a). *"One of the criminals who were hanged there was hurling abuse at Him, saying, 'Are You not the Christ? Save Yourself and us!' But the other answered, and rebuking him said, 'Do you not even fear God, since you are under the same sentence of condemnation? And we indeed are suffering justly, for we are receiving what we deserve for our deeds; but this man has done nothing wrong.' And he was saying, 'Jesus remember me when You come in Your kingdom!' And He said to him, 'Truly I say to you, today you shall be with Me in Paradise'"* (Luke 23:39-43).

> When wronged, I am compelled to ask myself:
> "Am I being asked to forgive as much as Christ
> was so very willing to forgive?"

"Jesus, knowing that the Father had given all things into His hands, and that He had come forth from God and was going back to God, got up from supper, and laid aside His garments; and taking a towel, He girded Himself. Then He poured water into the basin, and began to wash the disciples' feet and to wipe them with the towel with which He was girded. So He came to Simon Peter. He said to Him, 'Lord, do You wash my feet?' Jesus answered and said to him, 'What I do you do not realize now, but you will understand hereafter.' Peter said to Him, 'Never shall You wash my feet!' Jesus answered him, 'If I do not wash you, you have no part with Me.' Simon Peter said to Him, 'Lord, then wash not only

my feet, but also my hands and my head'" (John 13:3-9). Peter had not only forsaken Him at the time of His crucifixion but also had cursed and denied Him three times.

The above scripture implies that Jesus also washed the feet of Judas even though He knew he would very soon betray Him. Would my pride or my anger allow me to do as Christ did? There would be no pride or anger involved if I lived according to Jesus' teaching and example. How loving and kind are the examples of forgiveness of our merciful savior! *"Just as the Son of Man did not come to be served, but to serve, and to give His life a ransom for many" (Matthew 20:28).*

You Wash My Feet

You wash my feet, oh Lord, My God?
But no: You wash my all!
But only when I learned to trust,
And heed Your loving call.

And now, so clean, my heart can heed
Your Holy Spirit's words.
I'll be Your servant until my death,
As with "Your towel" I'm gird.

Oh Lord, the peace that fills my heart
When I obey Your will;
You calm me with Your words of love,
And anxious moments, still.

I long to see that place prepared
Where faithful saints will bask;
But may I wash your servants' feet
Until we meet at last!

This poem is dedicated to Mr. and Mrs. John Trimble who are ever ready to wash the feet of others.

My very deepest love and gratitude goes to Jay Conner, who lovingly set this poem to music. Jay and his precious wife, Carol, are of the mindset to live their lives paying it forward; and that is what this song expresses and should be the aim of every Christian. The song is available at www.rjstevensmusic.com/product/you-wash-my-feet/.

Following is a helpful pattern of servitude: every Lord's Day, early in the morning, Jay and Carol send a texted song concerning Jesus' death on the cross to nieces, nephews, and loved ones. This is so very good to consider before going to worship, as our minds are then already filled with His gift of love.

> "To sum up, all of you be harmonious, sympathetic,
> brotherly, kindhearted, and humble in spirit;
> not returning evil for evil or insult for insult,
> but giving a blessing instead;
> for you were called for the very purpose
> that you might inherit a blessing."
> —1 Peter 3:8-9

A heartbreaking and deeply sorrowful, but triumphant, journal entry by David Ditter on12/23/2016:

Dr. McBroom spoke with us tonight and has informed us that Rhonda's tabernacle is soon to be rendered useless as a place in which her spirit may dwell. No trial will accept a patient with bowel blockage and the blockage is not singularly located, which, if it were, it might have been surgically removed. Any other treatment that the doctor would provide would only serve to make Rhonda sicker and unable to enjoy any acceptable quality of life and would not add any meaningful extension to her carnal life. So, at some point in the near future, Rhonda's spirit will return to The One who gave it. The suffering will end, the daystar that has arisen in her life will shine as bright as can be. We will all give thanks to God for the life that He gave her and the many blessings she has received and given. Rhonda has learned to trust in the Lord with all her heart and that faith will redound to the glory of the Father, through whom all blessings flow. I had hoped and prayed that I might find the mercy I longed for, just as Paul received when Epaphroditus was sick, rather than have sorrow upon sorrow, that Rhonda might find that mercy. But God's ways are far higher than mine and His mercy is far greater than I can fathom. Besides that, it is far better to be with the Lord and I'm thankful to God for the peace and comfort I find in my confidence that He will receive her into everlasting habitations. Until that time comes, we will seek to give her all the comfort and love one can give. I know I've thanked you all for your love and compassion, your prayers to God and your encouraging faith and hope, but I find it impossible to thank you enough, so, thank you so much and may God bless you according to his great mercy. Praise God and give thanks for his great and holy Name, Name above all names, and His precious, beloved, only begotten Son, Jesus the Christ.

Be Still My Soul

Be still, my soul; the Lord is on thy side.
Bear patiently the cross of grief or pain;
Leave to thy God to order and provide…
In every change He faithful will remain.
Be still my soul, thy best, thy heavenly friend
Through thorny ways leads to a joyful end.

Be still, my soul; when dearest friends depart,
And all is darkened in the vale of tears.
Then shalt thou better know His love, His heart;
Who comes to soothe thy sorrow, and thy fears.
Be still my soul, the waves and winds shall know
His voice who ruled them while He dwelt below.

Be still my soul, the hour is hastening on,
When we shall be forever with the Lord;
When disappointment, grief and fear are gone,

Sorrow's forgot, love's purest joys restored.
Be still my soul, when change and tears are past,
All safe and blessed, O we shall meet at last.
–David T. Clydesdale/Jean Sibelius/
Katharina Von Schlegel

Chapter 6

Satan's Cruel Valleys
That Lead to Eternal Punishment

The title of this chapter alone makes it unappealing, as it should be. However, many aspects of the devil's cunning devices will be profitable for us to consider more carefully reconsider. These "Holy Spirit-inspired" warnings are not only necessary for us to heed, but they are also beneficial for us to be familiar with if we are to assist others who may be confused or disobedient. God exhorts us to help snatch others from the fire!

Too, one of our most important responsibilities is teaching our children the value of adhering to God's Word to avoid the painful rewards of disobedience. How heart-wrenching it would be to observe our children wavering in their service to God.

> *"Behold, the Lord's hand is not so short That it cannot save: Nor is His ear so dull That it cannot hear. But your iniquities have made a separation between you and your God, And your sins have hidden His face from you so that He does not hear."*
> *—Isaiah 59:1-2*

May we never allow this "separation" to apply to us!

God has very clearly and amply warned us concerning the deceiver, accuser, and slanderer. By doing this, He then allows us the liberty to have control of our soul's destination. He wants us to serve Him because of our abundant love and gratitude for Him, not because He has forced us. *"And if I give all my possessions to feed the poor, and If I surrender my body to be burned, but do not have love, it profits me nothing"* (I Corinthians 13:3).

> *"May the Lord direct your hearts into the love of God and into the steadfastness of Christ."*
> *—2 Thessalonians 3:5*

God's desire is for our names to remain written in the Book of Life: However, Satan's desire for us to have them blotted out! It is our choice. What is my desire? I cast the deciding ballot!

*"Beloved, I urge you as aliens and strangers
to abstain from fleshly lusts which wage war against the soul."*
—1 Peter 2:11

The apostle Peter has given us a warning to be constantly ready to answer those who are misinformed or uninformed concerning God's Word. *"Who is there to harm you if you prove zealous for what is good? But even if you should suffer for the sake of righteousness, you are blessed. AND DO NOT FEAR THEIR INTIMIDATION, AND DO NOT BE TROUBLED, but sanctify Christ as Lord in your hearts, always being ready to make a defense to everyone who asks you to give an account for the hope that is in you, yet with gentleness and reverence"* (1 Peter 3:13-15). We may think adding to or taking from God's commandments is a great thing for "us" and "our children," and thereby must be approved by Him. The following scriptures disapprove of that kind of reasoning. Paul's admonition is: *"But I am afraid that, as the serpent deceived Eve by his craftiness, your minds will be led astray from the simplicity and purity of devotion to Christ"* (2 Corinthians 11:3). *"Every word of God is tested; He is a shield to those who take refuge in Him. Do not add to His words or He will reprove you, and you will be proved a liar"* (Proverbs 30:5-6).

> *"But I am afraid that, as the serpent deceived Eve by his craftiness, your minds will be led astray from the simplicity and purity of devotion to Christ"* (2 Corinthians 11:3). *"Every word of God is tested; He is a shield to those who take refuge in Him. Do not add to His words or He will reprove you, and you will be proved a liar"* (Proverbs 30:5-6).

ॐ

"If anyone advocates a different doctrine and does not agree with sound words, those of our Lord Jesus Christ, and with the doctrine conforming to Godliness, he is conceited and understands nothing; but he has a morbid interest in controversial questions and disputes

about words, out of which arise envy, strife, abusive language, evil sus-picions, and constant friction between men of depraved mind and de-prived of the truth, who suppose that godliness is a means of gain."
—1 Timothy 6:3-5

I should understand and teach others to understand that serving God is not about pleasing ourselves while here on earth: it is about loving and trusting Him enough to serve Him according to His wishes obediently. May we never allow the soul-destroying doctrines or practices of mor-tal man to lure us away from what is true and acceptable to God. Only when we obey His commands is God pleased.

"Whoever speaks, is to do so as one who is
speaking the utterances of God."
—1Peter 4:11a

&

"Now may the God who gives perseverance and encouragement
grant you to be of the same mind with one another
according to Christ Jesus, so that with one accord
you may with one voice glorify the God and Father
of our Lord Jesus Christ."
—Romans 15:5-6

Do I remember these passages so I can use them myself and teach them to others? And may we always remember God's admonition to the saints to speak with gentleness? And, how Satan loves to stir up quarrels! *"Beloved, while I was making every effort to write you about our common salvation, I felt the necessity to write to you appealing that you contend earnestly for the faith which was once for all handed down to the saints"* (Jude 3).

Note the need to contend earnestly for the faith, requiring correct knowledge of "the faith," while avoiding being lured into any quar-relsome conversation. The devil delights in joining angry, spiteful, de-grading, ungodly contentions!

As we mine for other nuggets to escape being duped by Satan, let us consider the following: "Now flee from youthful lusts and pursue righteousness, faith, love and peace, with those who call on the Lord from a pure heart. But refuse foolish and ignorant speculations, knowing that they produce quarrels. The Lord's bond-servant must not be quarrelsome, but be kind to all, able to teach, patient when wronged, with gentleness correcting those who are in opposition, if perhaps God may grant them repentance leading to the knowledge of the truth, and they may come to their senses and escape from the snare of the devil, having been held captive by him to do his will" (2 Timothy 2:22-26). This scripture is a goldmine, not only for us but also for our youth. Now we must ask ourselves: "is our home a home of righteousness, faith, love, and peace? Do we avoid being caught up in petty quarrels or degrading put-downs? Do we always speak to our wife or husband respectfully as we would like for our child/children to later speak to their mate(s)?" On the other hand, am I "gently helping our children come to their senses and to recognize youthful lusts and how to avoid them? And, now, what did I learn from this self-examination? Am I willing to rectify wrong if that is necessary, OR am I hiding behind, "It was their fault," or "they started it?" Either statement will be of little value on the day of reckoning.

If we find ourselves leaning toward ANY kind of worldliness, we give the devil permission to snare us. We may find ourselves being handed a bag of money as Judas was. When temptation first appeals to us, we have the choice of being like Judas and stealing from the bag, or we can overcome the temptation and continue to be respected and trusted. Or, when the devil tempts us to lie, we can do so and quickly lose our place of loyalty to God. Is stealing or lying worth the reward it brings? Or lust or gossip or any other evil allurement? ALL sin is of the devil. The only reward it brings about is suffering now, and if not repented of and restitution made if needed, even more excruciating in eternity. And eternity is just that! E T E R N I T Y!

Genesis records reveal what it cost Adam and Eve when Eve was deceived, and Adam also disobeyed (Genesis 3:1-19). Surely this should deter us from following in their footsteps. Am I prepared to answer God on the day of judgment, or will I want to hide as they did? God has made it very clear: hiding from Him is impossible. *"O God, it is You who knows my folly, and my wrongs are not hidden from You." (Psalm 69:5).*

"Simon Peter, a bond-servant and apostle of Jesus Christ, To those who have received a faith of the same kind as ours, by the righteousness of our God and Savior, Jesus Christ:

*Grace and peace be multiplied to you in the knowledge
of God and of Jesus our Lord;
seeing that His divine power has granted to us everything
pertaining to life and godliness, through the true knowledge of Him
who called us by His own glory and excellence.
For by these He has granted to us
His precious and magnificent promises,
so that by them you may become partakers of the divine nature,
having escaped the corruption that is in the world by lust."
—2 Peter 1:1-4*

Another beautiful, reassuring Biblical passage.

"Grace and peace" are multiplied to us "in the knowledge of God and His Son." God's blessing!

But be aware! We, the citizens of America, are, at present, faced with living in a country that is fast casting away peace as it turns away from God's Holy Word while erecting false idols of its own making; abortion and the promotion of gay rights being among the most abhorrent! The devil is at work and is winning this sinful battle! May we escape "the corruption that is in the world by lust!" However, even though spiritual decay is truly at work, we must be grateful to God we can live in this country and pray for its citizens and its leaders that they might change to live Godly lives in this present world!

The God Our Fathers Respected

The light of a nation that once worshiped God
Grows more dim with each passing day:
Satan is leading our nation to sin
And soon, it will forget how to pray.

The laws our forefathers respected
Are considered archaic, untrue:
Leaving way for hate, crime and violence!
A catastrophic course, if pursued!

God's truths and His plans are all perfect;
They embrace love, joy and peace.
If we turn back to God as our ruler and King,
Only then will the violence cease!

Due to the rapidly increasing threats facing most Christians in most of the world today, we may have to commit to allowing ourselves to be persecuted even unto death. If so, we must pray while on our cross that the persecutors will find forgiveness from God, just as Jesus prayed. Exemplifying Jesus, we will be able to submit to being spit upon, beaten, reviled, and crucified without complaint. God has given us examples to follow to ready our hearts and minds to comply willingly and lovingly with any persecution we may face. This calls to mind the following admonition: *"And if I give all my possessions to feed the poor, and If I surrender my body to be burned, but do not have love, it profits me nothing"* (I Corinthians 13:3).

> *"Blessed is a man who perseveres under trial;*
> *for once he has been approved,*
> *he will receive the crown of life*
> *which the Lord has promised to*
> *those who love Him."*
> —James 1:12

Our God of all wisdom and mercy,
Please fill our hearts with a burning desire
to search your scriptures daily:
Scriptures that will cause us to remain
diligent in our service to You,
even as You have called us to serve;
With steadfastness, humility, and adoration!
Not according to our will, Father,
but may our will become Thy will,
that we may flourish as trees planted by water:
Even throughout these days of spiritual turmoil.
Your truths are pivotal in guarding our hearts
from the cunning devices of the evil one!
Truths that will provide us with wisdom to
avoid and/or escape Satan's dark, sin filled valleys.
Our souls long for, and beg You for a better place,
"The place" You have lovingly prepared for Your own:
Your Holy mountain!

Chapter 7

From Earthly Valleys of Distress to God's Heavenly, Pain-Free Mountain Top

God's Mountain

We're striving to climb your mountain, dear Lord
To hear Your sweet angels sing praise;
To see those streets that are paved with pure gold,
And to live there forevermore days.

We want to scale your mountain, dear Lord,
To escape these valleys so deep.
To gratefully sing of your wonderful grace,
And to joyfully dwell there in peace.

We thank you, dear Lord for the hope you provide
For those who are climbing each day.
Our hope is made sure by your promise secure;
We'll find rest at the end of our way.

This poem is dedicated to Gerald and Kathy Hester, who are always at work to gain heaven and to assist others as they climb.

"The Lord is near to all who call upon Him,
To all who call upon Him in truth."
—Psalm 145:18

And now, may we draw near to God as we allow Him to renew and strengthen our spiritual understanding to a degree we may have never claimed before! Can we not claim this every time we studiously meditate on His Word? Do we not see some depth of truth we had not pondered before? God's Word is a never-ending call to study! The following scriptures are then only a call for more and more study of the pure Word: the Holy Bible!

"O send out Your light and Your truth,
let them lead me;
Let them bring me to Your holy hill (mountain, NIV)
And to Your dwelling places."
—Psalm 43:3
Amen

"In the beginning was the Word, and the Word was with God, and the Word was God. He was in the beginning with God. All things came into being through Him, and apart from Him nothing came into being that has come into being. In Him was life, and the life was the Light of men" (John 1:1-4). Christ's life, from the very beginning of time, as we know it, was the "Light of men."

"How blessed is he whose help is the God of Jacob,
Whose hope is in the Lord his God, Who made heaven
and earth, The sea and all that is in them;
Who keeps faith forever."
—Psalm 146:5-6

The following prophecies concerning Christ coming to earth and establishing His Church are meant for God's followers to undergird and forever seal their hope of salvation. God desires us to know His past, present, and future plans and shares His perfect scriptural blueprint. May we read these prophecies with deep gratitude in our hearts for their revelation and their preservation.

Prophecy: *"For a child will be born to us, a son will be given to us, and the government will rest on His shoulders; And His name will be called Wonderful Counselor, Mighty God, Eternal Father, Prince of Peace"* (Isaiah 9:6). This prophecy inspired hope, awe, and thanksgiving in the hearts of believers at the time Isaiah made it, and as it can, and should also, in ours!

Fulfilled: *"And she gave birth to her firstborn Son; and she wrapped Him in cloths, and laid Him in a manger, because there was no room for them in the inn"* (Luke 2:7). And what was formerly only hope has awesomely and lovingly become a reality! But, a royal baby, born in a stable and placed in a manger? What is God teaching us by this? This humble way of life followed our Savior to the cross! Are our priorities in line with this example?

Prophecy: *"Therefore the Lord Himself will give you a sign: "Behold, a virgin will be with child and bear a son, and she will call His name Immanuel" (Isaiah 7:14).*

Fulfilled: *"Now the birth of Jesus Christ was as follows: when His mother Mary had been betrothed to Joseph, before they came together she was found to be with child by the Holy Spirit" (Matthew 1:18).*

A child by the Holy Spirit? Only our God could provide this miraculous birth!

"Now all this took place to fulfill what was spoken by the Lord through the prophet: "BEHOLD, THE VIRGIN SHALL BE WITH CHILD AND SHALL BEAR A SON, AND THEY SHALL CALL HIS NAME IMMANU-EL," which translated means, "GOD WITH US." And Joseph awoke from his sleep and did as the angel of the Lord commanded him, and took Mary as his wife, but kept her a virgin until she gave birth to a son; and he called His name Jesus" (Matthew 1:22-25).

Deity has indeed left heaven to come to dwell on the earth to save sinful men!

AND, this baby is born a KING!
—Matthew 2:1-2

❧

"And the Word became flesh, and dwelt among us,
and we saw His glory, glory as of the only begotten
from the Father, full of grace and truth."
—John 1:14

Prophecy: *"A Redeemer will come to Zion. (Jerusalem) (Isaiah 59:20a).* *"As for me, I know that my Redeemer lives, And at the last He will take His stand on the earth" (Job 19:25).* How long ago was this prophecy revealed? And yet, it has now proven to be undeniably true!

Fulfilled: *"But when the fulness of time came, God sent forth His Son, born of a woman, born under the Law, so that He might redeem those who were under the Law, that we might receive the adoption as sons" (Galatians 4:4-5).* Lowly, sinful, undeserving mankind can now accept the blessed gift of being saved from our sins! Now we can become adopted sons! The Holy Spirit does not leave us to wonder how this can be done. Scripture does not leave us uninformed!

> If we're willing to deal with what He can show us about ourselves, He is willing to show us more than we could ever imagine about the God that He is. —Gary Henry

Angels notified the shepherds of Jesus birth: *"In the same region there were some shepherds staying out in the fields and keeping watch over their flock by night. And an angel of the Lord suddenly stood before them, and the glory of the Lord shone around them; and they were terribly frightened. But the angel said to them, 'Do not be afraid; for behold, I bring you good news of great joy which will be for all the people; for today in the city of David there has been born for you a Savior, who is Christ the Lord. This will be a sign for you: you will find a baby wrapped in cloths and lying in a manger.' And suddenly there appeared with the angel a multitude of the heavenly host praising God and saying, 'Glory to God in the highest, And on earth peace among men with whom He is pleased.' When the angels had gone away from them into heaven, the shepherds began saying to one another, 'Let us go straight to Bethlehem then, and see this thing that has happened which the Lord has made known to us.' So they came in a hurry and found their way to Mary and Joseph, and the baby as He lay in the manger'"* (Luke 2:8-16). *"The shepherds went back, glorifying and praising God for all they had heard and seen, just as had been told them"* (Luke 2:20).

> A beautiful star in
> the heavens so bright,
> Led shepherds to Jesus,
> in the manger that night.
> And today, there's a
> Star in the heavens above:
> This savior, named Jesus:
> our gift of God's love!

"And the city has no need of the sun
or of the moon to shine on it,
for the glory of God has illumined it,
and its lamp is the Lamb."
—Revelation 21:23

Like the shepherds, as we welcome this very precious baby Jesus, are we not also GLORIFYING and PRAISING God and also feeling the ultimate joy, awe, and excitement of this occasion; feeling the awesome wonder of knowing without a doubt; God has fulfilled this prophecy?

Christ dwelt among us and was tempted in all points as we are. In tempting Him, Satan quoted scripture, revealing his perfect knowledge of God's Word, just as he had in tempting Eve. Eve SAW him, as we cannot, but we are not without hope; we can discern his presence when tempted to sin. How good that Jesus was, and is, our example of perfection as we face temptations!

As prophesied, Jesus was to face suffering and death so that through loving obedience to His commands, we might be cleansed of our sins. We can "know" the peace and related blessings of being in a right relationship with Him.

Prophecy: *"Behold, My servant will prosper, He will be high and lifted up and greatly exalted. Just as many were astonished at you, My people, So His appearance was marred more than any man And His form more than the sons of men"* (Isaiah 52:13-14). And Jesus foretold His crucifixion: *"They were on the road going up to Jerusalem, and Jesus was walking on ahead of them; and they were amazed, and those who followed were fearful. And again He took the twelve aside and began to tell them what was going to happen to Him, saying, 'Behold, we are going up to Jerusalem, and the Son of Man will be delivered to the chief priests and the scribes; and they will condemn Him to death and will hand Him over to the Gentiles. They will mock Him and spit on Him, and scourge Him and kill Him, and three days later He will rise again'"* (Mark 10:32-34). And this was carried out exactly as He said it would be! And this FOR US: sinful men and women! How could it be that He would do this for us? He loved us and continues to love us so!

Fulfilled: *"The God of our fathers raised up Jesus, whom you had put to death by hanging Him on a cross. He is the one whom God exalted* to His right hand as a Prince and a Savior, to grant repentance to Israel, and forgiveness of sins" (Acts 5:30-31).

And: Prophecy: *"By His knowledge the Righteous One, My Servant, will justify the many, As He will bear their iniquities. Therefore, I will allot Him a portion with the great, And He will divide the booty with the strong; Because He poured out Himself to death, And was numbered with the transgressors; Yet He Himself bore the sin of many, And interceded for the transgressors" (Isaiah 53:11b-12).*

Can we not hear the cruelly severe suffering and painful agony in His voice as He asked, *"Father, forgive them; for they do not know what they are doing" (Luke 23:34).*

Fulfilled: *"As Moses lifted up the serpent in the wilderness, even so must the Son of Man be lifted up; so that whoever believes will in Him have eternal life" (John 3:14-15) (Also, Mark 15:16-26).*

> Please help me to remember, dear God,
> Your suffering Son, who died upon a tree:
> And teach me then, to lovingly forgive, and to forget,
> The ones who have wrongfully wounded me!

True believers will joyfully be obedient to His commands in order to obtain eternal life with Him.

NOTE: did Jesus believe His earthly suffering was worth the price He paid for being obedient to His Father's will? His answer, of course, is a very triumphant, Yes! He endured the dreaded, brutally cruel cross for "the joy" set before Him.

> *"Therefore, since we have so great a cloud of witnesses*
> *surrounding us, let us also lay aside every encumbrance*
> *and the sin which so easily entangles us,*
> *and let us run with endurance the race that is set before us,*
> *fixing our eyes on Jesus, the author and perfecter of faith,*
> *who for the joy set before Him endured the cross,*
> *despising the shame,*
> *and has sat down at the right hand of the throne of God."*
> —Hebrews 12:1-2

We, too, can experience this same kind of joy as we are welcomed to live for Him!

Prophecy *"For you will not abandon my soul to Sheol (the grave, NIV); nor will You allow Your Holy One to undergo decay"* (Psalm 16:10).

Fulfilled: *"Brethren, I may confidently say to you regarding the patriarch David that he both died and was buried, and his tomb is with us to this day. And so, because he was a prophet and knew that GOD HAD SWORN TO HIM WITH AN OATH TO SEAT one OF HIS DESCENDANTS ON HIS THRONE, he looked ahead and spoke of the resurrection of the Christ, that HE WAS NEITHER ABANDONED TO HADES (grave, NIV) NOR DID His flesh SUFFER DECAY"* (Acts 2:29-31).

NOTE: After three days in the grave, the Holy Spirit reveals not only to His apostles but to us details concerning His triumphant resurrection! May we share in the joy of this predetermined event that sealed the promise of our resurrection from the grave (Matthew 28:1-15). Praise God for this revelation!

Before leaving this thought, let's consider the guards placed at the tomb of Jesus: *"Pilate said to them, 'You have a guard; go, make it as secure as you know how.' And they went and made the grave secure, and along with the guard they set a seal on the stone.* (This scripture alludes to the chief priests and the Pharisees being included in securing the grave.) *Now after the Sabbath, as it began to dawn toward the first day of the week, Mary Magdalene and the other Mary came to look at the grave. And, behold, a severe earthquake had occurred, for an angel of the Lord descended from heaven and came and rolled away the stone and sat upon it. And his appearance was like lightning, and his clothing as white as snow. The guards shook for fear of him and became like dead men. The angel said to the women, 'Do not be afraid; for I know that you are looking for Jesus who has been crucified. He is not here, for He has risen, just as He said. Come, see the place where he was lying'"* (Matthew 27:65-28:6).

Can we not feel the fear the guards felt when the earth shook and the angel of the Lord appeared? They "became like dead men!" How could they not believe this was the Christ they had been attempting to guard? (but failed)! And how did Satan take control of this situation? First through MONEY, then with DECEIT! Two of his most effective tools! *"Now while they were on their way, some of the guard came into the city and reported to the chief priests all that had happened. And when they had assembled with the elders and consulted together, they gave a large sum of money to the soldiers, and said, 'You are to say, 'His disciples came by night and stole Him away while we were asleep'"* (Matthew 28:11-13). May we take note of how easy it was for Satan (using the chief priests and elders) to lure them with money, causing them to become deceivers. It would be good for us if we remember to consider that wisdom is required when offered money as a reward.

Did Pilate's wife believe the story provided by the guards (Matt 27:19)? This is not revealed to us. But what about me? How deep is my faith concerning the resurrection? *"Now may the God of hope fill you with all joy and peace in believing, so that you will abound in hope by the power of the Holy Spirit"* (Romans 15:13). We must have a belief that perseveres. Peter believed in Christ before the resurrection but was willing to deny Christ three times. After the resurrection, he was then ready to die for him. We gain that type of belief only through meditation and study of the scriptures.

Before returning to His Father, Jesus chose and prepared apostles (ones sent) to continue to carry out the teaching concerning His offer of salvation from sin. *"And when day came, He called His disciples to Him and chose twelve of them, whom He also named apostles"* (Luke 6:13).

"He said to them, it is not for you to know the times or epochs (dates, NIV) which the Father has fixed by His own authority; but you will receive power when the Holy Spirit has come upon you; and you shall be My witnesses both in Jerusalem, and in all Judea and Samaria, and even to the remotest part of the earth."
—Acts 1:7-8

And following, this:

Among His most precious earthly gifts: the establishment of His Church (Acts 2:1-42). And in this passage of scripture, we are given the keys to become members of His Church. As members, we gain spiritual peace, and the hope of heaven can be our "undeserved" reward!

"And He put all things in subjection under His feet, and gave Him as head over all things to the church,

which is His body, the fullness of Him
who fills all in all."
—Ephesians 1:22-23

ℬ

Our Prayer

Our Father Who reigns from heaven,
Hallowed be Your Holy and matchless Name.
Your kingdom, the Church, has come,
Your will has, and is, being done
On earth as it was, and is, in heaven.
You provide us each day with our daily bread
And lovingly forgive our transgressions
As we forgive those who trespass against us.
You do not lead us into temptation
As You tempt no one;
But rather, You deliver us from the evil one,
Because You love Your children
and provide a way of escape.
You, Oh God, are our King;
the Ruler of the Kingdom;
The power and the Glory forever and ever.
Amen.

Lest we forget or fail to appreciate His suffering for us, Christ instituted the Lord's supper, the table of remembrance (Matthew 26:26-29; Luke 22:14-20; 1 Corinthians 10:16-17).

To faithful Christians, it is a precious gift that Jesus asks us to meet together as His chosen family, with Him, on the first day of the week. This gathering together was to remember the body Christ allowed to be sacrificed and the blood that He shed that was required for forgiveness of sin. May our hearts overflow with gratitude as we remember the unjust, mercilessly cruel crucifixion: His body so cruelly beaten and spat upon, and His blood that flowed so freely for our condemning sins.

The First Day of The Week

This is a wonderful day of love, dear Lord,
This day of worshiping You!
And a wonderful day of grace, bestowed,
Remembering what Christ suffered through.

This is a day of deep gratitude, Lord,
As we ponder Your pure love for us;
A day our hearts are at peace, dear Lord,
As in Thee, we place "all" of our trust.

How you have blessed us this day, dear Lord!
As You have, each "precious day" of our lives,
We can cross that "last valley" with peace in our hearts,
As our souls, in Your daily care, will survive. Amen.

ℰℴ

And as King David requested:
"Let the words of my mouth
And the meditation of my heart
Be acceptable in Your sight,
O Lord, my rock and my Redeemer."
—Psalm 19:14

ℰℴ

The Lord's Supper

When we meet in sweet communion
Where the feast divine is spread;
Hearts are brought in closer union
While partaking of the bread.

"God so loved" what wondrous measure!
Loved and gave the best of heav'n
Bought us with that matchless treasure,
Yea, for us His life was giv'n.

Feast divine, all else surpassing,
Precious blood for you and me,
While we sup, Christ gently whispers:
"Do this in my memory."

Precious feast all else surpassing,
Wondrous love for you and me,
While we feast Christ gently whispers:
"Do this in my memory."
–Tillit S. Teddlie

સ

Until we realize that the self-indulgent "worship" that passes for reverence today is an insult to God, it's not likely that we'll seek Him as we should.
—Gary Henry

How does my love for Him and my fellow man compare to the love God has shown for me? A very sobering, soul searching, challenging thought.

And finally, His ascension to be with His Father in heaven.

"And He led them out as far as Bethany, and He lifted up His hands and blessed them. While He was blessing them, He parted from them and was carried up into heaven. And they, after worshiping Him, returned to Jerusalem with great joy, and were continually in the temple praising God" (Luke 24:50-53).

સ

"Then I saw a new heaven and a new earth; for the first heaven and the first earth passed away, and there is no longer any sea. And I saw the holy city, new Jerusalem, coming down out of heaven from God, made ready as a bride adorned for her husband. And I heard a loud voice from the throne, saying, "Behold the tabernacle of God is among men, and He will dwell among them, and they shall be His people, and God Himself will be among them, and He will wipe away every tear from their eyes; and there will no longer be any death;

there will no longer be any mourning, or crying, or pain; the first things have passed away." —Revelation 21:1-4

God will "DWELL" among them! How can I take all of this passage in without being humbled and experiencing great joy as the apostles did after Christ's departure; and, consequently, striving to be lovingly and faithfully obedient!

His Created Beauty

What beauty we see in Your mountains!
Your lakes! Your moon and Your stars!
If we cannot describe all their beauty,
Then what of heaven? That is soon to be ours.

And the words of salvation You gave us?
Their beauty overflows from our souls!
Your wisdom! Your grace! Your deep love for us;
Makes Your heaven, our "attainable" GOAL!

℘

"When Christ, who is our life, is revealed, then you also will be revealed with Him in glory."
—Colossians 3:4

℘

*"Beloved, now we are children of God,
and it has not appeared as yet what we will be.
We know that when He appears, we will be like Him,
because we will see Him just as He is."*
—1 John 3:2

*"For we know that if the earthly tent which is our house is torn down,
we have a building from God, a house not made with hands,
eternal in the heavens. For indeed in this house we groan,
longing to be clothed with our dwelling from heaven,
inasmuch as we, having put it on, will not be found naked.
For indeed, while we are in this tent, we groan, being burdened,*

because we do not wish to be unclothed but to be clothed,
so that what is mortal will be swallowed up by life.
Now He who prepared us for this very purpose is God,
who gave to us the Spirit as a pledge (or downpayment)."
—2 Corinthians 5:1-5

ဢ

The Open Door

The old tired fisherman, caught in a storm,
Longs to reach the distant tree lined shore,
Where warmth and love and rest await,
At his home, with an open door.

And so it is with the tired weary soul
Of him, who longs to reach his heavenly shore,
Where love and boundless joy await,
And his God! Who waits with an open door!

Dedicated to Rod and Paula Hovater, who are daily
assisting children, the elderly and many, many others to
safely reach that open door. God's dedicated servants!

ဢ

"Therefore, my beloved brethren, be ye steadfast,
immovable, always abounding in the work of the Lord,
knowing that your toil is not in vain in the Lord."
—1 Corinthians 15:58

ဢ

God's Love and Grace

Oh God, please fill my heart with beauty
Until it spills from heart to pen,
That I may share Your grace with others,
Until I've said my last Amen!

Thank you for this day You gave us;
And for our souls that yearn for You:
And may we live each precious moment,
With only thoughts of pleasing You.

Then when Jesus comes to take us
From this earth, to realms above;
Where we can sing Your praise forever,
Your gift to us? Your precious home of love!

What could this earthly home e'er give us
That would match this gift from You?
Do not let the "evil one" deceive us
By saying your promises are not true!

Only from your Book of wisdom, help us gather
All Your matchless truths that set us free;
That prepare us with Your grace, to enter,
Your home of untold beauty; there to dwell eternally!

Dedicated to precious friends, John and Rosemary
Brown who have lovingly encouraged me as I wrote.
They too, are dedicated servants!

And now we are strengthened as we are blessed to be able to read the final two journal entries by David Ditter. He valiantly continues to persevere through this devastating valley he is continuing to mine, even after Rhonda's passing.

This deep valley can be escaped in time, but the memory of it will last a lifetime.

Addressing Rhonda's "Victory in Jesus" - Wednesday, January 11, 2017

"So, this is another day that the Lord has made, rejoice and be glad in it, for this is the day that my dear sweet, young bride, your sister, daughter, mother and friend, Rhonda Lynn Ditter has secured her victory in Jesus and over death. I, and I suspect all of you, are thankful to God for all these years we had

Rhonda, to love and to hold and to watch her live a life well-lived and to give glory to the Father for every blessing, just as we do. She was a servant, and did not view her service as anything other than what was expected of her Master, although we tend to view such service with admiration, wishing that I was also "that" servant. I do not deserve the least of all His mercies, although He did heap to me many mercies, as he blessed me with a very special gift in Rhonda. I praise Him and I give honor and glory to Him for all of her good works. I am thankful for the rest that she can finally enjoy and for the glory that she will have, that cannot be compared with the suffering she has endured. Rhonda's spirit passed peacefully from her tabernacle very early this morning and returned to the Father of spirits. How wonderful it is when we reach that place of peace and rest."

Can we not feel David's peace and deep gratitude that Rhonda was not living in Satan's valley with no hope? Let God be praised! She was God's servant child!

I'll Fly Away

Some glad morning when this life is o'er,
I'll fly away;
To a home on God's celestial shore,
I'll fly away.

When the shadows of this life have grown,
I'll fly away;
Like a bird from prison bars have flown,
I'll fly away.

Just a few more weary days and then,
I'll fly away;
To a land where joys shall never end,
I'll fly away.

I'll fly away, O glory, I'll fly away;
When I die, Hallelujah, by and by,
I'll fly away.
—Albert E Brumley

(The above song is a favorite of David's, and was used in Rhonda's memorial service.)

∽

*"One thing I have asked from the Lord,
that I shall seek: That I may dwell in the
house of the Lord all the days of my life,
To behold the beauty of the Lord,
And to meditate in His temple."*
—Psalm27:4

∽

*"He who overcomes, I will make him a pillar
in the temple of My God, and he will not go out
from it anymore; and I will write on him the name
of My God, and the name of the city of My God, the
new Jerusalem, which comes down out of heaven
from My God, and My new name."*
—Revelation 3:12

∽

And: the final journal entry of David Ditter, dated 1/12/2017:

"My observations, during my short time on earth, lead me to believe there is no greater power than that of "love". What can be so beautiful about observing this power, as we observed it in Rhonda, is that it does its work throughout the lifespan of the living soul that possesses it; Be it for a few short years, or, be it for several decades, it moves mountains and heals the souls of many, but it does so softly and tenderly. God is found in the still, small voice, not in the whirlwind and the work of love, though far greater in power, works that way. I know I've told you time and again how overwhelmed I have been by the love and support (manifested in so many different ways) during this time and how encouraged Rhonda was by your comments and your desire to encourage her in any possible way. May God receive the glory and may he so richly bless you and me with the power of love and provide everything you need. We love you."

Blest Be The Tie That Binds

Blest be the tie that binds
Our hearts in Christian love;
The fellowship of kindred minds
Is like to that above.

Before our Father's throne,
We pour our ardent prayers;
Our fears, our hopes, our aims are one,
Our comforts and our cares.

We share our mutual woes;
Our mutual burdens bear;
And often for each other flows
The sympathetic tear.

When we asunder part,
It gives us inward pain;
But we shall still be joined in heart,
And hope to meet again.
—John Fawcett

"Rejoice in the Lord always; again I will say, rejoice!
Let your gentle spirit be known to all men.
The Lord is near. Be anxious for nothing,
but in everything by prayer and supplication
with thanksgiving let your requests be made
known to God. And the peace of God,
which surpasses all comprehension,
will guard your hearts and your minds in Christ Jesus."
—Philippians 4:4-7

Today I am one day nearer home than ever before. One day nearer the dawning when the fog will lift, mysteries clear, and all question marks straighten up into exclamation points! I shall see the King.
—Vance Havner

As we have learned from God's Holy Word, the real joy of life is not just enduring and overcoming each valley, but also the ultimate joy of peacefully looking forward to heaven.

As Job, may we valiantly persevere so we can claim this glorious blessing God so graciously offers to His faithful servants! And may the beaconing light that emits from His throne lead us to His dwelling place; His holy mountain top!

Each Step I Take

Each step I take my Savior goes before me,
And with His loving hand He leads the way.
And with each breath I whisper, "I adore Thee."
Oh, what joy to walk with Him each day!

At times I feel my faith begin to waver,
When up ahead I see a chasm wide.
It's then I turn and look upon my Savior.
I am strong when He is by my side.

I trust in God, no matter come what may,
For life eternal is in His hand:
He holds the key that opens up the way
That will lead me to the promised land.

Each step I take, I know that He will guide me,
To higher ground He ever leads me on.
Until some day the last step will be taken,
Each step I take just leads me closer home.
—W. Elmo Mercer

ॐ

*Now may the God of hope
fill you with all joy and peace in believing,
so that you will abound in hope by the power of the Holy Spirit.
(Romans 15:13)*

ॐ

This is the God we love, we adore,
Our Father, our Hope and our Friend;
Who promises rest at the end of our way,
As from our valleys, we transcend!
Then we'll dwell securely on His mountaintop,
Where our spirits will live without end!
Oh! the joy we will know, because God loves us so;
Our Father, our Hope, and our Friend!

ॐ

"Now may the God of peace Himself sanctify you entirely;
and may your spirit and soul and body
be preserved complete, without blame at the coming of our Lord
Jesus Christ.
Faithful is He who calls you, and He also will bring it to pass."
—1 Thessalonians 5:23-24

In closing the book, I thank God for allowing me to finish this "labor of love" and, hopefully, see it in print before my life ends. My prayer is that I have not misrepresented our mighty GOD in any way and that it has been presented with, and is received with, "gentleness and reverence" as God desires (I Peter 3:15).

My final tribute is to the following children and young adults: God's present and future servants! Caleb, Isaac, and Samuel Hester, Leon and Rinoa Mauldin, Isaiah Mahn, and Davis Lindsey. They, among others, are responsible for making my aging heart know new bounds of love and immense joy!